Diet recommendations for chronic constipation

Please check these recommendations always with a nutrition consultant, therapist, doctor or dietician. The recipes and the list of ingredients are supporting the conventional medical therapy.
The calorie disclosures of fresh ingredients (fruit and vegetables) vary according to quality and time of harvest. The contents were checked by a dietician and a nutrition consultant for the Traditional Chinese Medicine (TCM).

Author:
©2017 Josef Miligui
www.ebns.at

Source:
The lists are created from the EBNS database for nutritional counseling. The database is used by dietitians, therapists and doctors for advising the patient / client.

Literature:
The specialist literature and the training documents of the German and Austrian dietary and traditional Chinese medicine serve as a knowledge base. We have used the documents as a basis of knowledge, adapted it to our experience and completed them.
http://di-book.com

Title Photo:
©2008 Erika Weixlbaumer

Production and publishing:
BoD – Books on Demand, Norderstedt
ISBN 9783743189249

(Book: E017)

Diet recommendations for DIETETICS - Gastrointestinal tract - Small intestine and large intestine - Chronic constipation

1 Treatment strategy 5
2 Avoid 6
3 Breakfast 6
4 Snack 7
5 Lunch 7
6 Afternoon 9
7 Dinner 9
8 Any time 11
9 Recipes 13
   9.1 Antipasti 13
   9.2 Artichoke soup 13
   9.3 Asparagus Cream Soup 14
   9.4 Avocado with lemon 15
   9.5 Barley and vegetable soup 16
   9.6 Barley mash with steamed pear 16
   9.7 Barley soup 17
   9.8 Basic recipe for a beef broth (clear) 18
   9.9 Basic recipe for a fish broth 18
   9.10 Basic recipe for a reissue soup (Congee) 19
   9.11 Basic recipe for a vegetable soup, nutritious 20
   9.12 Basmati rice + Zucchini tofu dish 21
   9.13 Beef broth 21
   9.14 Bilberry - curd cheese with Acai powder 22
   9.15 Bircher-muesli with yogurt, nuts and apple 23
   9.16 Black root with yogurt 23
   9.17 Blueberry puree 24
   9.18 Boiled celery salad with exotic spices 24
   9.19 Breakfast with cheese 25
   9.20 Broccoli and Parmesan spread on toast bread 26
   9.21 Broccoli cream soup 27
   9.22 Carrot and millet bake with apple compote 27
   9.23 Carrot and potato rucola sandwich 28
   9.24 Carrot drink 29
   9.25 Celery and potato cream soup 30
   9.26 Cold cherry soup with curd cheese dumpling 30
   9.27 Colorful Tuscan bean soup 31
   9.28 Compote from plums 32
   9.29 Compote of pears 32

9.30	Corn coffee with cardamom	33
9.31	Cottage cheese with steamed fruit	33
9.32	Couscous Salad	34
9.33	Cranberry yogurt mix	34
9.34	Cream cheese substitute	35
9.35	Cucumber soup	35
9.36	Delicately spiced zucchini with tomatoes	36
9.37	Exotic lenses	37
9.38	Fennel and potato gratin	38
9.39	Fennel with roasted walnuts	39
9.40	Figs with mozzarella and honey	39
9.41	Fish soup with rosemary	40
9.42	Fried apple	41
9.43	Frozen pineapple juice	42
9.44	Fruit juice	42
9.45	Grapefruit juice	42
9.46	Halibut with tomato and garlic sauce	43
9.47	Hearty polenta mash	44
9.48	Hearty winter breakfast	44
9.49	Hot water with grape juice	45
9.50	Lasagne with tofu cream	45
9.51	Lettuce with fresh cheese	46
9.52	Lettuce with vinegar dressing	47
9.53	Marinated cod on pumpkin puree	47
9.54	Millet with pears	48
9.55	Millet with shiitake mushrooms and avocado	49
9.56	Miso soup with tofu	50
9.57	Nettle-chard soup	50
9.58	Noodle casserole with plugs and peaches	51
9.59	Oat flakes with aromatic spices	52
9.60	Oatmeal soup with spring onion and carrots	52
9.61	Olive oil with lemon juice	53
9.62	Oven potatoes with celery-curd cheese (quark)	53
9.63	Oyster mushrooms with asparagus	54
9.64	Pancakes with spinach and parmesan	55
9.65	Pear compote	56
9.66	Pear juice	56
9.67	Plum Cake	56
9.68	Porcino mushroom-smoked tofu on toast bread	57
9.69	Potato cream with herbs and fresh cheese	58
9.70	Potato pancakes	59
9.71	Potato with dandelion salad	59
9.72	Potato-basil soup	60

9.73	Potato bags with wild herbs and tomato sauce	61
9.74	Potatoes with wild garlic-curd cheese	62
9.75	Pumpkin curry	63
9.76	Pumpkin soup	63
9.77	Quick zucchini soup	64
9.78	Radish with sugar	65
9.79	Raw celery salad	65
9.80	Refreshing cucumber soup with potatoes	66
9.81	Rhubarb cake with sprinkles	66
9.82	Ribbon noodles with leaf spinach	67
9.83	Rice with parsnips	68
9.84	Rice with stewed vegetables	69
9.85	Roasted barley patties	69
9.86	Rosemary Potatoes	70
9.87	Russian kasha with white cabbage	71
9.88	Salmon on tomato-spinach	71
9.89	Scrambled eggs with leaf salad olives and tomatoes	72
9.90	Scrambled eggs with rocket and herbs	73
9.91	Sliced chicken with walnuts and sherry	74
9.92	Spicy avocado cream with cottage cheese	75
9.93	Spicy Tofu Vegetable Pan	75
9.94	Spinach with Tahini	76
9.95	Strawberry soup with melons	77
9.96	Strawberry yoghurt and almond puree mix	77
9.97	Tea from anise	78
9.98	Tea from coriander	78
9.99	Tea from elderberry blossom tea	78
9.100	Tea from fenugreek (Trigonella foenum-graecum)	79
9.101	Tea from ginger with honey	79
9.102	Tea from ground	80
9.103	Tea from Marjoram	80
9.104	Tea mixture against intestinal inertia	80
9.105	Thick pea soup	81
9.106	Tomato soup	82
9.107	Turkey breast with vegetables (Asian)	82
9.108	Vanilla cream with berries	83
9.109	Vanilla pudding	84
9.110	Vegetable bowl with Provencal pistou	84
9.111	Vegetable juice	85
9.112	Vegetable semolina soup	86
9.113	Warming carrot soup	87
9.114	Wheat semolina with olives-herb-sauce and salad	87
9.115	Wild garlic cream soup	88

9.116 Wild garlic dumplings 89
9.117 Wild garlic-scrambled eggs-breads 90
10 Effects of food 91
    10.1 Use ingredients: recommendable 91
    10.2 Use ingredients: yes 91
    10.3 Use ingredients: little 96
    10.4 Do not use contra-acting foods 98
11 Herbs and their effects 99
    11.1 Basil (fresh) 99
    11.2 Savory 99
    11.3 Nettles 99
    11.4 Dill 99
    11.5 Chervil dried 99
    11.6 Coriander 99
    11.7 Herbs various 99
    11.8 Cress 99
    11.9 Chives 100
    11.10 Lovage 100
    11.11 Dandelion (young plants) 100
    11.12 Marjoram 100
    11.13 Oregano fresh 100
    11.14 Parsley 100
    11.15 Peppermint 100
    11.16 Rosemary 100
    11.17 Sage 101
    11.18 Sorrel 101
    11.19 Blackthorn (Sloe) 101
    11.20 Black caraway 101
    11.21 Thyme dried 101
    11.22 Lemongrass 101
    11.23 Lemon Balm (fresh) 101
12 Basics of Nutrition 102
    12.1 Nutrition 102
    12.2 Recipes 104
    12.3 Foodstuffs 104
    12.4 Herbs 105
13 Other dietic-books 106

1 Treatment strategy

Diet rich in fiber, sufficient fluid intake.
Plums, figs and apricots, bran (with plenty of liquid), flaxseed (with

plenty of liquid), rhubarb, sauerkraut, beetroot (also available as juice), Indian flea seed, wholecorn pasta, full rice, millet, oats, wholemeal, tubers, potatoes , Legumes, pears, peaches, cherries, dried fruit, figs, wholemeal bread.

2 Avoid

White bread, pasta, bananas, chocolate, red wine, black tea.

3 Breakfast

kkal. per serving

Avocado with lemon	289
Barley and vegetable soup	281
Barley soup	265
Bircher-muesli with yogurt, nuts and apple	383
Blueberry puree	10
Boiled celery salad with exotic spices	165
Breakfast with cheese	593
Broccoli and Parmesan spread on toast bread	148
Carrot and potato rucola sandwich	94
Carrot drink	143
Compote from plums	22
Compote of pears	122
Corn coffee with cardamom	3
Cottage cheese with steamed fruit	214
Couscous Salad	338
Cream cheese substitute	526
Cucumber soup	95
Fried apple	408
Fruit juice	175
Hearty polenta mash	262
Hearty winter breakfast	678
Hot water with grape juice	87
Millet with pears	213
Millet with shiitake mushrooms and avocado	559
Miso soup with tofu	51
Oat flakes with aromatic spices	280
Oatmeal soup with spring onion and carrots	134
Pear compote	100
Plum Cake	502
Potato cream with herbs and fresh cheese	217
Potato pancakes	893

Rhubarb cake with sprinkles 475
Rice with parsnips 206
Rosemary Potatoes 188
Scrambled eggs with leaf salad olives and tomatoes 419
Scrambled eggs with rocket and herbs 360
Spicy avocado cream with cottage cheese 613
Strawberry yoghurt and almond puree mix 134
Thick pea soup 123
Vanilla cream with berries 278
Vanilla pudding 254
Vegetable semolina soup 198
Wheat semolina with olives-herb-sauce and salad 244
Wild garlic-scrambled eggs-breads 360

4 Snack

Carrot and potato rucola sandwich 94
Cream cheese substitute 526
Figs with mozzarella and honey 415
Plum Cake 502
Rhubarb cake with sprinkles 475

5 Lunch

Antipasti 100
Artichoke soup 142
Asparagus Cream Soup 240
Avocado with lemon 289
Barley and vegetable soup 281
Barley mash with steamed pear 113
Barley soup 265
Basmati rice + Zucchini tofu dish 145
Beef broth 124
Bircher-muesli with yogurt, nuts and apple 383
Black root with yogurt 424
Blueberry puree 10
Boiled celery salad with exotic spices 165
Broccoli and Parmesan spread on toast bread 148
Broccoli cream soup 98
Carrot and millet bake with apple compote 349
Carrot and potato rucola sandwich 94
Carrot drink 143
Celery and potato cream soup 112
Cold cherry soup with curd cheese dumpling 320

Colorful Tuscan bean soup	249
Compote from plums	22
Compote of pears	122
Corn coffee with cardamom	3
Cottage cheese with steamed fruit	214
Couscous Salad	338
Cranberry yogurt mix	57
Cream cheese substitute	526
Cucumber soup	95
Delicately spiced zucchini with tomatoes	203
Exotic lenses	143
Fennel and potato gratin	147
Fennel with roasted walnuts	342
Fish soup with rosemary	271
Fried apple	408
Frozen pineapple juice	29
Fruit juice	175
Halibut with tomato and garlic sauce	319
Hearty polenta mash	262
Hot water with grape juice	87
Lasagne with tofu cream	301
Lettuce with fresh cheese	802
Lettuce with vinegar dressing	67
Marinated cod on pumpkin puree	201
Millet with pears	213
Millet with shiitake mushrooms and avocado	559
Miso soup with tofu	51
Nettle-chard soup	52
Noodle casserole with plugs and peaches	442
Oatmeal soup with spring onion and carrots	134
Oven potatoes with celery-curd cheese (quark)	304
Oyster mushrooms with asparagus	316
Pancakes with spinach and parmesan	329
Pear compote	100
Pear juice	180
Potato cream with herbs and fresh cheese	217
Potato pancakes	893
Potato with dandelion salad	162
Potato-basil soup	95
Potato bags with wild herbs and tomato sauce	417
Potatoes with wild garlic-curd cheese	254
Pumpkin curry	193
Pumpkin soup	104

Quick zucchini soup 41
Radish with sugar 46
Raw celery salad 590
Refreshing cucumber soup with potatoes 148
Ribbon noodles with leaf spinach 722
Rice with parsnips 206
Rice with stewed vegetables 166
Roasted barley patties 398
Rosemary Potatoes 188
Russian kasha with white cabbage 250
Salmon on tomato-spinach 364
Scrambled eggs with leaf salad olives and tomatoes 419
Scrambled eggs with rocket and herbs 360
Sliced chicken with walnuts and sherry 304
Spicy avocado cream with cottage cheese 613
Spicy Tofu Vegetable Pan 241
Spinach with Tahini 150
Strawberry soup with melons 87
Strawberry yoghurt and almond puree mix 134
Thick pea soup 123
Tomato soup 100
Turkey breast with vegetables (Asian) 535
Vegetable bowl with Provencal pistou 137
Vegetable semolina soup 198
Warming carrot soup 133
Wheat semolina with olives-herb-sauce and salad 244
Wild garlic cream soup 231
Wild garlic dumplings 905
Wild garlic-scrambled eggs-breads 360

6   Afternoon

Carrot and potato rucola sandwich 94
Figs with mozzarella and honey 415
Plum Cake 502
Rhubarb cake with sprinkles 475
Vanilla pudding 254

7   Dinner

Artichoke soup 142
Asparagus Cream Soup 240
Barley and vegetable soup 281
Barley soup 265

Basmati rice + Zucchini tofu dish	145
Beef broth	124
Black root with yogurt	424
Blueberry puree	10
Boiled celery salad with exotic spices	165
Broccoli cream soup	98
Carrot drink	143
Celery and potato cream soup	112
Cold cherry soup with curd cheese dumpling	320
Compote from plums	22
Compote of pears	122
Corn coffee with cardamom	3
Cranberry yogurt mix	57
Cream cheese substitute	526
Delicately spiced zucchini with tomatoes	203
Exotic lenses	143
Fennel and potato gratin	147
Fennel with roasted walnuts	342
Fish soup with rosemary	271
Fried apple	408
Frozen pineapple juice	29
Fruit juice	175
Halibut with tomato and garlic sauce	319
Hearty polenta mash	262
Hot water with grape juice	87
Lasagne with tofu cream	301
Lettuce with vinegar dressing	67
Millet with pears	213
Millet with shiitake mushrooms and avocado	559
Miso soup with tofu	51
Oven potatoes with celery-curd cheese (quark)	304
Pancakes with spinach and parmesan	329
Pear compote	100
Pear juice	180
Porcino mushroom-smoked tofu on toast bread	169
Potato with dandelion salad	162
Potato-basil soup	95
Pumpkin curry	193
Pumpkin soup	104
Quick zucchini soup	41
Radish with sugar	46
Raw celery salad	590
Refreshing cucumber soup with potatoes	148

Ribbon noodles with leaf spinach	722
Rice with parsnips	206
Rice with stewed vegetables	166
Roasted barley patties	398
Rosemary Potatoes	188
Russian kasha with white cabbage	250
Salmon on tomato-spinach	364
Sliced chicken with walnuts and sherry	304
Spicy avocado cream with cottage cheese	613
Spicy Tofu Vegetable Pan	241
Spinach with Tahini	150
Strawberry soup with melons	87
Thick pea soup	123
Tomato soup	100
Turkey breast with vegetables (Asian)	535
Vegetable bowl with Provencal pistou	137
Vegetable semolina soup	198
Warming carrot soup	133
Wheat semolina with olives-herb-sauce and salad	244
Wild garlic cream soup	231
Wild garlic dumplings	905
Wild garlic-scrambled eggs-breads	360

8 Any time

Avocado with lemon	289
Bilberry - curd cheese with Acai powder	237
Bircher muesli with yogurt, nuts and apple	383
Blueberry puree	10
Carrot drink	143
Compote from plums	22
Compote of pears	122
Corn coffee with cardamom	3
Cranberry yogurt mix	57
Frozen pineapple juice	29
Fruit juice	175
Hot water with grape juice	87
Lettuce with vinegar dressing	67
Miso soup with tofu	51
Pear compote	100
Pear juice	180
Potato with dandelion salad	162
Radish with sugar	46

Rice with parsnips 206
Strawberry yoghurt and almond puree mix 134
Tea from anise 2
Tea from ginger with honey 4
Tea from Marjoram 0

9 Recipes

(recommendable) = You can use more.
(little) = You should use less than specified or omit.

9.1 Antipasti

Improves blood circulation, anti-inflammatory, relieves pain. Diuretic, promotes digestion, reduces blood pressure. antioxidativ, antibacterial, affects anorexia, improves digestion, flatulence, stomach weakness.
Cooking time approx. 40 min
Calories p. portion: 100
3 portions
Allergens: -

Quantity of ingredients
Olive oil 1 table spoon / 15g. (yes)
Coriander 1/2 teaspoon / 2g. (yes)
Aubergine 1 piece / 300g. (yes)
Lemon peel 1/2 piece / 3g. (yes)
Lemon juice 1 table spoon / 10g. (yes)
Pepperoni 1 piece / 5g. (yes)
Basil (fresh) 8 leaves / 5g. (yes)
Zucchini 5/8 oz / 200g. (recommended)
Tomato 4 pieces / 200g. (yes)
Salt 1 pinch / 0,5g. (little)

Cooking instructions:
Preheat the oven to 250 degrees Celsius and bake the hot peppers until the bowl becomes dark (about 20 minutes). Cover the hot peppers with a clear film and allow to cool. Peel the skin and cut into strips about 2 cm wide. Cut tomatoes in half and spread with oil in slices of aubergine and bake in the oven at 200 degrees golden brown (about 10 minutes) Fry the zucchini slices in the grill pan (without fat).
Mix everything together, mix the marinade of olive oil, salt and lemon peel and pour over the vegetables, sprinkle with coriander. Leave for 1 hour.

9.2 Artichoke soup

Detoxifying, supports urination, regulates digestion, stimulates appetite, gentle laxative, forcing spleen, promotes weight loss. Strengthens gastrointestinal function, expands blood vessels, prevents cancer.
Cooking time approx. 40 min

Calories p. portion: 142
3 portions
Allergens: GLN

Quantity of ingredients
Corn flour 1 table spoon / 10g. (little)
Sesame paste (Tahini) 1 table spoon / 10g. (yes)
Turmeric (yellow root) 1 pinch / 1g. (yes)
Basic recipe for a vegetable soup (nutritious) 1 cup / 250g. (yes)
Artichoke 4 pieces / 400g. (yes)
Nutmeg 1 pinch / 0,5g. (yes)
Sesame, white 1 teaspoon / 10g. (recommended)
Lemon 1/4 piece / 8g. (yes)
Onion (shallot) 1 piece / 20g. (yes)
Butter Bio 1 table spoon / 20g. (little)
Salt 1 pinch / 0,5g. (little)
Lemon peel 1/4 piece / g. (yes)

Cooking instructions:
Boil the artichokes in 2 liters of water with salt until the outer leaves are light removable. Remove leaves and flower center (fibrous) so that only the soil remains.
Melt the butter, cut the onion into small pieces and steam gently; add some cornmeal, nutmeg; brew with vegetable soup; add salt, a little lemon peel and juice, turmeric and artichoke bottoms, cook gently and puree; Season with Tahini and sprinkle with sesame before serving.

9.3 Asparagus Cream Soup

Diuretic, improves blood circulation, prevents cancer, laxative, antiparasitic, stimulates liver function, good to fight loss of appetite, flatulence, rheumatism, heartburn.
Cooking time approx. 45 min
Calories p. portion: 240
2 portions
Allergens: ACG

Quantity of ingredients
Asparagus (green or white) 5/8 oz / 200g. (yes)
Rapeseed oil 2 table spoons / 30g. (yes)
Wheat flour 2 table spoons / 10g. (yes)
Chicken yolk 1 piece / 25g. (little)
Cow's milk (whole milk 3.5% fat) 1 table spoon / 15g. (yes)

Sour cream 15% fat 1 table spoon / 15g. (yes)
Pepper (ground) 1 pinch / 0,5g. (yes)
Nutmeg 1 pinch / 0,5g. (yes)
Parsley 2 table spoons / 20g. (yes)
Salt 1 pinch / 1g. (little)
Water 2 cup / 500g. (yes)
Lemon juice 1 teaspoon / 2g. (yes)

Cooking instructions:
Wash and peel the asparagus.
Heat water, a little lemon juice and pinch of salt till it boils. Tie the asparagus spears together.
Add the asparagus peel to the cooking water and bring to the boil.
Add the asparagus and cook on low heat for about 20 minutes.
Then remove the asparagus bunches and pour the broth through a sieve.
For the roux, heat the oil in a saucepan, add the flour and sauté until it is colorless, slowly top up with the asparagus sauce and simmer for 10 minutes.
Cut the asparagus spears into pieces about 3 cm long and place them to the soup.

Just before serving, bring the soup to the boil again.
Mix the egg yolk with the milk and sour cream.
Remove the pot from the heat and stir in the egg yolk and milk mixture.
Season with pepper and nutmeg, decorate with the chopped parsley and serve immediately.

9.4   Avocado with lemon

Good to fight insomnia, inflammation, swelling, pain and itching. Is calming.
Cooking time approx. 5 min
Calories p. portion: 289
1 portions
Allergens: -

Quantity of ingredients
Avocado 1/2 piece / 120g. (yes)
Lemon juice 1/2 piece / 10g. (yes)
Salt 1 pinch / 1g. (little)

Cooking instructions:
Halve the avocado, remove the core, add the lemon juice, salt a little and eat with a spoon.

9.5 Barley and vegetable soup

Supports urination, detoxifying, promotes spleen and liver, reduces blood pressure, strengthens immune system, prevents cancer, reduces radiation damage, promotes digestion, helps to digest fat, harmonizes
Cooking time approx. 2 hours
Calories p. portion: 281
3 portions
Allergens: AGL

Quantity of ingredients
French beans Handful / 30g. (recommended)
Shiitake, dried 1/8 oz / 4g. (yes)
Pepper (ground) 1 pinch / 0,5g. (yes)
Parsley 1 teaspoon / 3g. (yes)
Butter Bio 1 teaspoon / 3g. (little)
Water 1 cup / 250g. (yes)
Celery sticks 2 branches / 20g. (yes)
Barley 1 cup / 120g. (yes)
Onion (shallot) 1 piece / 20g. (yes)
Sunflower oil 1 table spoon / 10g. (little)
Carrot 2 pieces / 150g. (yes)
Peas, green 5/8 lbs - 8oz / 250g. (yes)
Tomato 1 piece / 50g. (yes)
Salt 1 pinch / 1g. (little)
Cumin (Caraway seed) 1 knife tip / 0,5g. (yes)

Cooking instructions:
Soak the barley in the evening for the next day. Soak the mushrooms separately at the next day. Brown onion and cumin in oil, then boil with water. Add the chopped vegetables, some salt, the barley and the shiitake mushrooms and cook everything to a thick soup. At the end, season with pepper, parsley and a little butter.

9.6 Barley mash with steamed pear

Promotes digestion, supports urination, promotes spleen, diuretic, forcing spleen, relaxes, promotes perspiration.
Cooking time approx. 25 min
Calories p. portion: 114

5 portions
Allergens: A

Quantity of ingredients
Barley 1 cup / 120g. (yes)
Sugar cane sugar 1/2 teaspoon / 5g. (little)
Pear 1 piece / 200g. (yes)
Water 10 cups / 1200g. (yes)
Salt 1 pinch / 1g. (little)
Ginger fresh 2 slices / 2g. (yes)
Cardamom 3 capsules / 1g. (yes)

Cooking instructions:
Grind coarse the barley and roast it dry. Add hot water, add ginger and cardamom and let it swell to a pulp in low heat. Peel and dice the pear and boil for 10 minutes with a little water. At the end, add the stewed pear, a little butter and sweetener.

Variant: If you want to go fast, you can use barley flakes instead of shot.

9.7 Barley soup

Diuretic, forcing spleen, supports urination, stimulates liver function, antioxidative, promotes digestion, detoxifying, reduces blood lipids, stimulates, dissolves stagnation.
Cooking time approx. 25 min
Calories p. portion: 265
2 portions
Allergens: A

Quantity of ingredients
Salt 1 pinch / 1g. (little)
Ginger fresh 1/2 teaspoon / 1g. (yes)
Barley 1 cup / 120g. (yes)
Parsley 2 table spoons / 30g. (yes)
Olive oil 1 table spoon / 10g. (yes)
Water 1 1/2 cups / 240g. (yes)

Cooking instructions:
Roast the barley in the pan, then grind it to the ground, and boil with water, some salt and ginger to a mash. Before serving add oil and parsley. Variant: You can add a better taste to the dish if you cook it with prepared vegetable or meat broth.

9.8 Basic recipe for a beef broth (clear)

Strengthens muscles, tendons and bones, reduces blood pressure, strengthens immune system, stimulates digestion, reduces pain, promotes digestion, diuretic. Rosemary stimulates digestion.
Cooking time approx. 4-8 hours
Calories p. portion: 114
10 portions
Allergens: O

Quantity of ingredients
Water 3,3 lbs / 1300g. (yes)
Leek 1 piece / 200g. (yes)
Clove 2 pieces / 2g. (yes)
Rosemary 1 pinch / 1g. (yes)
Carrot 3 pieces / 210g. (yes)
Pimento 6 pieces / 12g. (yes)
Beef meatbones 5/8 oz / 200g. (little)
Anise (Common Fennel) 2 pieces / 1g. (yes)
Parsnip 2 pieces / 300g. (yes)
Ginger fresh 1/2 teaspoon / 5g. (yes)
Salt 1 teaspoon / 5g. (little)
Juniper berry 8 pieces / 6g. (recommended)
Vinegar (Red wine vinegar) 1 dash / 3g. (yes)
Lovage 1 stem / 15g. (yes)
Beef soup meat 1,1 lbs / 500g. (little)

Cooking instructions:
Heat water, a dash of red wine vinegar, some juniper berries, a little rosemary, bones and meat till it boils; add carrot, parsnip, leek, ginger, lovage, clove, allspice, star anise and a little salt; simmer for 4-8 hours then strain.
Refrigerate for later use.

9.9 Basic recipe for a fish broth

Strengthens the kidneys, promotes watering, reduces blood pressure, strengthens immune system, prevents cancer, reduces radiation damage. Low in cholesterol and protein rich. Improves blood circulation, stimulates
Cooking time approx. 40 min
Calories p. portion: 128
5 portions
Allergens: DLO

Quantity of ingredients
Bay leaf 2 leaves / 2g. (yes)
Celery root 1/4 lbs - 4oz / 120g. (yes)
Olive oil 1 table spoon / 10g. (yes)
Lemon 1/2 piece / 50g. (yes)
Peppercorns 3 pieces / 2g. (yes)
Leek 2 inches / 10g. (yes)
Water 2 cup / 450g. (yes)
Fish pieces mixed (fresh water) 3/4 lbs / 300g. (yes)
White wine 1/2 cup / 125g. (little)
Carrot 2 pieces / 150g. (yes)

Cooking instructions:
Fry celery, chopped carrots and leeks in olive oil, add bay leaf and peppercorns, add pieces of fish and sauté
briefly. Add water, add little white wine or lemon. Simmer gently for 30 minutes. Skim off the resulting foam several
 times. In the end, sift the ingredients through a cloth.
Refrigerate for later use

9.10 Basic recipe for a reissue soup (Congee)

Low fat content, for the drainage of the body overweight and high blood pressure.
Cooking time approx. 2-4 hours
Calories p. portion: 140
3 portions
Allergens: -

Quantity of ingredients
Rice variety any 1 cup / 120g. (little)
Water 6 cups / 700g. (yes)

Cooking instructions:
Cook rice and water in a ratio of about 1: 6. The amount of water determines the thickness of the mash (matter of taste).
Put the rice in a saucepan with a heavy lid. It is important to simmer the rice after a short boil on the slightest flame, otherwise it burns.
Boil the rice for 2-4 hours. The longer he cooks, the more he strengthens.
If you want to eat the dish for breakfast, you can put the rice on just before bedtime.
To be on the safe side, you should first check the behavior of your pot

and cooker under observation for a similar amount of time, so that nothing burns.
Refrigerate for later use.

9.11 Basic recipe for a vegetable soup, nutritious

Reduces blood pressure, strengthens immune system, prevents cancer, forcing spleen, dissolves stagnation, promotes weight loss. Good to fight immunodeficiency, high blood pressure, depressions, diabetes, diarrhea, reduces blood lipids.
Cooking time approx. 2-3 hours
Calories p. portion: 48
5 portions
Allergens: L

Quantity of ingredients
Salt 1 pinch / 1g. (little)
Parsnip 3/8 lbs - 6oz / 150g. (yes)
Thyme dried 1 pinch / 1g. (yes)
Lovage 1 table spoon / 3g. (yes)
Bay leaf 2 leaves / 1g. (yes)
Olive oil 1 table spoon / 4g. (yes)
Ginger fresh 1/2 teaspoon / 2g. (yes)
Juniper berry 6 pieces / 6g. (recommended)
Lemon 1/2 piece / 25g. (yes)
Celery root 1 cup / 100g. (yes)
Water 3 cups / 650g. (yes)
Carrot 3 pieces / 200g. (yes)
Onion white 1 piece / 60g. (yes)

Cooking instructions:
Cut the vegetables into cubes.
Heat oil in hot pot, fry shortly onions and vegetables.
Add cold water, then add ginger, bay leaf and lemon juice.
Season with juniper, thyme and lovage. Cover for 2 - 3 hours on a low heat and simmer.
The used vegetables should be thrown away.
The basic recipe serves as a soup base and to refine vegetables, legumes or cereals.
If you want to eat vegetable soup immediately, add the desired vegetables half an hour before.
Refrigerate for later use.

9.12 Basmati rice + Zucchini tofu dish

Diuretic, supports urination, harmonizes spleen and stomach, reduces flatulence, good to fight body overweight and high blood pressure. Antioxidativ, promotes digestion, perspiration, reduces blood lipids, forcing spleen.
Cooking time approx. 20 min
Calories p. portion: 146
4 portions
Allergens: E

Quantity of ingredients
Zucchini 1 piece / 700g. (recommended)
Ginger fresh 1/2 teaspoon / 4g. (yes)
Rice Basmati 1/2 cup / 60g. (little)
Olive oil 2 table spoons / 6g. (yes)
Coriander 1/2 teaspoon / 4g. (yes)
Soy Tofu 5/8 lbs - 8oz / 250g. (yes)
Water 3 cups / 200g. (yes)

Cooking instructions:
Cut tofu cubes and marinate with olive oil, tamari, crushed coriander and ginger. Leave at least 1 hour.
Cook Basmati rice with the water. You can season with onion and cardamom.
Roast zucchini and tofu in pan in the hot oil for approx. 5-7 min.
Serve rice and tofu on a plate.
Add the parsley.
Can also be used as a salad for the home and on the go.

9.13 Beef broth

Warming and nourishing, forces.
Cooking time approx. 2-6 hours
Calories p. portion: 125
7 portions
Allergens: L

Quantity of ingredients
Parsley root 1 piece / 150g. (yes)
Celery root 1 inch / 25g. (yes)
Onion white 1 piece / 50g. (yes)
Bay leaf 2-3 leaves / 2g. (yes)
Coriander 1/2 teaspoon / 2g. (yes)

Wakame 1 inch / 1g. (yes)
Water 4 cup / 1000g. (yes)
Parsley 1 stem / 10g. (yes)
Carrot 2 pieces / 100g. (yes)
Ginger fresh 1 inch / 2g. (yes)
Beef meatbones 2 pieces / 0g. (little)
Beef meat 1,1 lbs / 500g. (little)
Turmeric (yellow root) 1 pinch / 1g. (yes)
Lemon 2 daches / 2g. (yes)

Cooking instructions:
In a saucepan with water (enough to cover the meat), add a few drops of lemon juice, a little turmeric, beef and bones, heat till it boils and simmer for a while; then pour away the whole broth, clean the pot, rinse off meat and bones with hot water (this will save you from foaming) and put it back to the saucepan with hot water (amount as you like); add a good pinch of turmeric, carrot, celery, parsley root to the pot; add onion, bay leaves, coriander, a piece of sliced ginger, a strip of wakame, a stalk of parsley; boil everything together and simmer for 2-6 hours (if the meat is to be used otherwise, take it out of the broth after 1 1/2 - 2 hours, as soon as it is cooked, the bones are returned to the broth); When the cooking time is over, pour the broth through a sieve and discard all ingredients.

Notes: The longer the broth has cooked, the warmer but more nourishing it is. It is after cooling for 3-4 days in the refrigerator durable. The broth can be drunk hot or used as a base for soups with cereals, potatoes and fresh vegetables.

9.14 Bilberry - curd cheese with Acai powder

Good to fight weakness, belching, diabetes, acute or chronic obstruction of the bowel, skin problems. Laxative, antibacterial effect. Antioxidant.
Cooking time approx. 10 min
Calories p. portion: 238
2 portions
Allergens: GH

Quantity of ingredients
Almond 1 table spoon / 5g. (yes)
Cinnamon ground 1 pinch / 0,5g. (yes)
Acai powder 2 teaspoons / 5g. (recommended)

Sugar cane sugar 1 table spoon / 9g. (little)
Curd cheese 20% 5/8 lbs - 8oz / 250g. (yes)
Blueberry 5/8 oz / 200g. (yes)
Orange juice 2 table spoons / 10g. (little)
Maple syrup 1 table spoon / 5g. (little)

Cooking instructions:
Rinse the blueberries in a sieve and pat dry gently. Drizzle with orange juice and maple syrup and stir in the Acai powder.
Roast the almond sticks in a frying pan until golden brown until they are fragrant and allow to cool on a plate. Dust with a little cinnamon.
Stir quark and sugar until smooth.
Layer alternately the quark with the marinated blueberries in glasses and garnish with the almonds.

9.15 Bircher-muesli with yogurt, nuts and apple

Fibre-rich, relieves constipation, strengthens immune system, forcing spleen, promotes weight loss. Good to fight immunodeficiency, loss of appetite.
Cooking time approx. 2 hours and more
Calories p. portion: 383
1 portions
Allergens: AGH

Quantity of ingredients
Oat flakes (whole grain) 2 table spoons / 20g. (recommended)
Lemon 1 table spoon / 10g. (yes)
Yogurt (natural, 3.5% fat) 6 table spoons / 80g. (yes)
Apple (sour) 1 piece / 170g. (little)
Hazelnuts 1 table spoon / 10g. (yes)
Acerola fruit nectar or powder 1/2 teaspoon / 1g. (little)
Muesli 2 table spoons / 20g. (recommended)

Cooking instructions:
Soak oatmeal in the yogurt for several hours in the fridge. Add rubed nuts, lemon juice, acerola, grated apple. For
sweets, raisins can be used.

9.16 Black root with yogurt

Stimulates kidney, bladder and forces the cleaning of the body. In the physiological sense, they generally stimulate the glands in the organism. Good to fight acute or chronic constipation of the intestine.

Rich in Vitamins and trace elements.
Cooking time approx. 20 min
Calories p. portion: 424
2 portions
Allergens: AG

Quantity of ingredients
Herbs various 2 table spoons / 6g. (yes)
Yogurt (natural, 1.5% fat) 4 table spoons / 80g. (yes)
Salt 1 pinch / 1g. (little)
Multi-grain bread (gray bread) 6 slices / 120g. (recommended)
Herbs various 1 table spoon / 8g. (yes)
Salsify 1 lbs / 400g. (yes)

Cooking instructions:
Peel the salsify and simmer in salted water until tender. Pour away the water, cool the salsify and cut it to size.
Cover with yoghurt and sprinkle with fresh herbs. Serve with the bread.
You can also use the salsify from the conserve.

9.17 Blueberry puree

Bilberry is laxative. Clove dissolves stagnation. Cinnamon powder heats stomach and spleen, improves blood circulation.
Cooking time approx. 10 min
Calories p. portion: 10
1 portions
Allergens: -

Quantity of ingredients
Water 1 cup / 250g. (yes)
Clove 1 piece / 1g. (yes)
Cinnamon ground 1 pinch / 0,1g. (yes)
Blueberry 1/2 oz / 20g. (yes)

Cooking instructions:
Boil blueberries with cinnamon and clove in water for 10 minutes. Remove the cinnamon and clove. Puree. Sweet as desired.

9.18 Boiled celery salad with exotic spices

Forcing spleen, relieves diarrhea, antibacterial, blood-forming, blood detoxifying, reduces inflammation, diuretic, improves blood circulation.
Cooking time approx. 30 min

Calories p. portion: 166
4 portions
Allergens: GLMNO

Quantity of ingredients
Lemon juice 1 piece / 40g. (yes)
Sesame oil 1 table spoon / 20g. (little)
Peppers powder 1 pinch / 1g. (yes)
Sour cream 15% fat 2 table spoons / 20g. (yes)
Salt 1 pinch / 1g. (little)
Pepper (ground) 1 pinch / 0,5g. (yes)
Onion white 1/2 piece / 25g. (yes)
Celery root 1 1/2 piece / 900g. (yes)
Vinegar (Apple vinegar) 1 dash / 3g. (yes)
Yogurt (natural, 3.5% fat) 1 cup / 250g. (yes)
Black caraway 1 pinch / 1g. (yes)
Mustard 1/2 teaspoon / 1g. (yes)
Apple (sour) 1/2 piece / 100g. (little)
Turmeric (yellow root) 1 pinch / 1g. (yes)
Lemongrass 1 pinch / 1g. (yes)

Cooking instructions:
Cook the peeled celeriac in thick slices and then cut into bite-sized strips.
Dressing: Mix a little yoghurt, sour cream, turmeric, sesame oil, pepper, lemongrass powder, finely chopped onion, a little mustard, salt, crushed black cumin, some cold water, lemon juice or vinegar; add the sour chopped apple, some rose paprika, the lukewarm celery and mix well; let it rest for 2 - 3 hours or overnight.
Ideal as a substitute for raw food

9.19 Breakfast with cheese

Good to fight weakness, stomach pressure, belching, diabetes, acute or chronic obstruction of the bowel, skin problems. Coffee supports urinating, stimulates appetite, detoxifying, increases blood glucose levels, harmonizes heart rhythm.

Cooking time approx. 10 min
Calories p. portion: 593
1 portions
Allergens: AGO

Quantity of ingredients
Whole grain bread 2 slices / 100g. (recommended)
Margarine 1/2 oz / 10g. (little)
Edam cheese 1 oz / 30g. (yes)
Water 1 cup / 120g. (yes)
Coffee 2 teaspoons / 4g. (yes)
Strawberry jam 1/2 oz / 20g. (little)
Curd cheese 20% 1/8 lbs - 2oz / 40g. (yes)

Cooking instructions:
Prepare coffee as usual. Avoid sugar or use sweetener. Cover the bread slices with margarine and put the cheese and marmalade on the breakfast table. Decorating decoratively increases your appetite.

9.20 Broccoli and Parmesan spread on toast bread

Good to fight loss of appetite, blood clotting, thyroid function, increase Vitamin B12, strengthen immune system, good to fight belching, diabetes, acute or chronic constipation, dissolves stagnation.
Cooking time approx. 15 min
Calories p. portion: 148
2 portions
Allergens: AG

Quantity of ingredients
Basil (fresh) 1 table spoon / 5g. (yes)
Broccoli 5/8 oz / 200g. (yes)
Yogurt (natural, 1.5% fat) 1 table spoon / 10g. (yes)
Parmesan 2 table spoons / 15g. (yes)
Lemon peel 1/2 teaspoon / 1g. (yes)
Toast bread (whole grain) 6 slices / 24g. (yes)
Pepper (ground) 1 pinch / 0,3g. (yes)
Salt 1 pinch / 1g. (little)
Chives 1 table spoon / 5g. (yes)
Curd cheese 20% 3 oz / 80g. (yes)

Cooking instructions:
Cook broccoli in a sieve insert over steam for 8 minutes until firm. Finely chop broccoli.
Mix the curd, yoghurt, parmesan and lemon peel well. Mix cheese cream with broccoli, basil and chives. Season the spread with salt and pepper. Serve on the crunchy toasted toast.

9.21 Broccoli cream soup

Strengthen your immune system, build and maintain healthy bones, teeth, hair and nails. Reduces blood pressure, strengthens immune system, prevents cancer, reduces radiation damage.
Cooking time approx. 30 min
Calories p. portion: 98
6 portions
Allergens: LO

Quantity of ingredients
Sage 1 teaspoon / 2g. (yes)
Broccoli 1,1 lbs / 500g. (yes)
Salt 1 pinch / 1g. (little)
Rosemary 1 teaspoon / 2g. (yes)
White wine 1/2 cup / 125g. (little)
Basic recipe for a vegetable soup (nutritious) 2 cup / 500g. (yes)
Onion white 1 piece / 50g. (yes)
Pepper (ground) 1 pinch / 0,5g. (yes)
Potato 2 pieces / 120g. (yes)
Olive oil 2 table spoons / 7g. (yes)
Carrot 2 pieces / 150g. (yes)
Water 1 cup / 50g. (yes)

Cooking instructions:
Add the olive oil to the pan, add the washed and cut broccoli, diced carrots and potatoes, sauté for a short time, add the chopped onion, fill with water, enough water to cover the vegetables at least 3 finger breadths. Add bouillon, salt, add a little bit of white wine, add the seasoned sage and rosemary.
Heat till it boils and then simmer on a small fire for about 25 minutes. Season with pepper, if necessary season with sea salt. Purée the soup.

9.22 Carrot and millet bake with apple compote

Promotes spleen and liver, reduces blood pressure, strengthens immune system, prevents cancer, reduces radiation damage, calms nerves and stomach, diuretic, good to fight chronic constipation of the intestine.
Cooking time approx. 1 hour
Calories p. portion: 350
7 portions
Allergens: CGH

Quantity of ingredients
Apple (sour) 4 pieces / 600g. (little)
Sugar brown 1 table spoon / 10g. (little)
Ginger fresh 2 teaspoons / 6g. (yes)
Water 1 cup / 300g. (yes)
Carrot 7/8 lbs / 400g. (yes)
Butter Bio 1 teaspoon / 4g. (little)
Sugar brown 2 table spoons / 20g. (little)
Yogurt (natural, 1.5% fat) 3/8 lbs - 6oz / 150g. (yes)
Chicken egg 4 pieces / 240g. (little)
Cow's milk (whole milk 3.5% fat) 2 cups / 450g. (yes)
Clove 2 pieces / 1g. (yes)
Lemon peel 1/2 piece / 2g. (yes)
Acerola fruit nectar or powder 1 teaspoon / 2g. (little)
Millet 5/8 oz / 200g. (recommended)
Almond puree 1/8 lbs - 2oz / 50g. (little)

Cooking instructions:
Preheat the oven to 100°C/212°F (with circulating air 8o°C/176°F, gas level 2).
Heat the milk with the millet till it boils, add lemon zest and sugar. Cover and simmer for 5 minutes, then simmer in a preheated oven for 20 minutes. Switch oven to medium heat.
Peel apples and cut into small pieces, boil with water, cloves and sugar for about 5 minutes.
Mix the millet in a bowl with the grated carrots, finely chopped ginger and acerola.
Mix the almond paste (or butter) with the hand mixer. Add egg yolk and stir everything to a smooth cream. Mix in sour cream. Add millet and carrots.
Beat the egg whites very stiff and lift them under the millet pulp. Brush out a baking dish with butter. Add the millet and bake in a preheated oven for 45 minutes on a low heat. Serve with the apple compote.

9.23 Carrot and potato rucola sandwich

Reduces inflammation, improves digestion, supports urination, lowers cholesterol, strengthens immune system, prevents cancer, good to fight constipation (Fibre-rich), dissolves stagnation.
Cooking time approx. 20 min
Calories p. portion: 94
4 portions
Allergens: AG

Quantity of ingredients
Whole grain bread 8 slices / 48g. (recommended)
Pepper (ground) 1 pinch / 0,2g. (yes)
Salt 1 pinch / 1g. (little)
Lemon peel 1/4 teaspoon / 1g. (yes)
Rucola 1/2 bunch / 100g. (yes)
Onion (spring onion) 1 piece / 20g. (yes)
Sour cream 15% fat 2 table spoons / 45g. (yes)
Carrot 1 piece / 50g. (yes)
Potato (mealy) 5/8 oz / 200g. (yes)

Cooking instructions:
Cook the potatoes gently, peel and squeeze through the potato press. Cook vegetable broth according to the basic recipe and remove a carrot after a short cooking time and finely crush with a fork.
Stir the potatoes, carrots, grated lemon zest and sour cream into a smooth cream.
Mix carrot and potato cream with finely chopped rocket salad. Season the spread with salt and pepper and spread the bread. Sprinkle with the finely chopped young onions.

9.24 Carrot drink

Promotes spleen and liver, reduces blood pressure, strengthens immune system, prevents cancer, reduces radiation damage, diuretic, building up, eye-enhancing, detoxifying, nerve-strengthening.
Cooking time approx. 15 min
Calories p. portion: 143
1 portions
Allergens: H

Quantity of ingredients
Carrot 7/8 lbs / 200g. (yes)
Water / 50g. (yes)
Honey 1/2 teaspoon / 2g. (little)
Almond puree 1 teaspoon / 3g. (little)
Millet flakes 1 table spoon / 10g. (recommended)

Cooking instructions:
Sprinkle millet flakes with 50 ml of cold water and let it swell for 10 minutes.
Juice the fresh carrots or use 200 ml. carrot juice. Puree the millet flakes, carrot juice, almond paste and honey with the blender.

9.25 Celery and potato cream soup

Reduces blood pressure, strengthens immune system, promotes weight loss. Good to fight immunodeficiency, loss of appetite, flatulence, depressions, diabetes, diarrhea, improves digestion.
Cooking time approx. 45 min
Calories p. portion: 113
4 portions
Allergens: GL

Quantity of ingredients
Olive oil 1 table spoon / 10g. (yes)
Basic recipe for a vegetable soup (nutritious) 3 cups / 700g. (yes)
Potato 5/8 oz / 200g. (yes)
Nutmeg 1 pinch / 0,5g. (yes)
Ground 1 pinch / 0,5g. (yes)
Lemon peel 1/4 piece / 1g. (yes)
Onion white 1/2 piece / 25g. (yes)
Salt 1 pinch / 1g. (little)
Parsley 1 table spoon / 8g. (yes)
Crème fraiche cheese 2 table spoons / 20g. (little)

Cooking instructions:
Heat the olive oil in a saucepan lightly. Fry the onions very gently in a mild heat. Pour with vegetable stock according to the basic recipe. Cover and cook for 15 minutes.
Add curd-cut potato, celery, nutmeg, cumin and lemon zest. Spice with salt and cook for 12 minutes. Potatoes and celery should be soft. Remove the lemon peel.
Puree the soup with crème fraiche using a blender. Season the soup with salt.
Arrange the soup in portions with the chopped parsley.

9.26 Cold cherry soup with curd cheese dumpling

Improves blood circulation, reduces inflammation, good to fight weakness, belching, diabetes, acute or chronic obstruction of the bowel. Laxative, stimulates digestion, cleans the intestinal flora.
Cooking time approx. 2 hours and more
Calories p. portion: 320
2 portions
Allergens: GO

Quantity of ingredients
Vanilla sugar natural 1 package / 1g. (little)
Sugar brown 1 table spoon / 10g. (little)
Lemon peel 1 pinch / 1g. (yes)
Cinnamon ground 1 pinch / 0,5g. (yes)
Sour cream 15% fat 1/8 lbs - 2oz / 50g. (yes)
Curd cheese 20% 1/4 lbs - 4oz / 100g. (yes)
Agar agar (kelp) 1/2 teaspoon / 1,5g. (yes)
Cherry compote 7/8 lbs / 450g. (yes)

Cooking instructions:
Strain the cherry compote.
Finely puree half of the cherries with the cherry juice using a blender and pass through a sieve.
Stir agar agar powder with cold water until smooth.
Bring the cherry puree to boil while stirring.
Mix in the agar-agar and cook the cherry puree for 1 minute while stirring.
Spread hot cherry puree on two soup plates.
Sprinkle the remaining cherries into the soup.
Cool down cherry soup for 2 hours until lightly gelled.
Use the hand mixer to stir the cord cheese, sour cream, sugar, vanilla sugar, cinnamon and lemon zest into a smooth, firm cream.
From the cream with the tablespoon, prick small dumplings and put them into the cherry soup.

9.27 Colorful Tuscan bean soup

Promotes digestion, helps to digest fat, supports urination, reduces blood pressure, diuretic, calms the stomach.
Cooking time approx. 2 hours
Calories p. portion: 249
3 portions
Allergens: L

Quantity of ingredients
Olive oil 2 table spoons / 50g. (yes)
Pepper (ground) 1 pinch / 0,5g. (yes)
Salt 1 pinch / 1g. (little)
Celery sticks 1 stick / 10g. (yes)
Kidney beans (red) 1/8 lbs - 2oz / 50g. (recommended)
Fennel seeds ground 1/2 teaspoon / 1g. (yes)
Lentils 1 oz / 25g. (recommended)

Chickpeas 1 oz / 25g. (recommended)
Garlic 1 clove / 3g. (yes)
Water 2 1/4 cups / 500g. (yes)
Tomato 2 pieces / 100g. (yes)
Basil (fresh) 5-7 leaves / 3g. (yes)

Cooking instructions:
Soak legumes, boil and puree. Add vegetables, spices, herbs and oil and cook gently for 2 hours.
Variation: Sweet chestnuts give the dish a special Italian touch.

9.28 Compote from plums

Cancer preventive effect, dehydrates the body, stimulates digestion and binds fats in the intestine.
Cooking time approx. 10 min
Calories p. portion: 22
2 portions
Allergens: -

Quantity of ingredients
Cinnamon ground 1 pinch / 1g. (yes)
Water 1 1/2 cups / 240g. (yes)
Plums 1/4 lbs - 4oz / 100g. (recommended)

Cooking instructions:
Boil plums in water until soft. Sprinkle with a little cinnamon.

9.29 Compote of pears

Pear benefits digestion, supports urination. Cocoa forces liver, strengthens the muscles, strengthens the defense. Good to fight fungi infections.
Cooking time approx. 10 min
Calories p. portion: 122
4 portions
Allergens: -

Quantity of ingredients
Anise (Common Fennel) 1/2 teaspoon / 1g. (yes)
Vanilla pod 1 pinch / 1g. (yes)
Pear 4 pieces / 800g. (yes)
Water 1 cup / 280g. (yes)
Cocoa 1 pinch / 1g. (yes)

Cooking instructions:
Boil pears (organic - with peel), aniseed, vanilla, chili soft. Sprinkle with cocoa.

9.30 Corn coffee with cardamom

Diuretic, forcing spleen, supports urination, relaxes, reduces fat.
Cooking time approx. 5 min
Calories p. portion: 3
1 portions
Allergens: -

Quantity of ingredients
Cereal coffee 1 table spoon / 15g. (yes)
Water 1 cup / 120g. (yes)
Cardamom 2 cores / 1g. (yes)

Cooking instructions:
Boil water, coffee, sugar and cardamom. Let it set for one min before drinking.

9.31 Cottage cheese with steamed fruit

Good to fight loss of appetite, promotes digestion, supports urination.
Cooking time approx. 20 min
Calories p. portion: 214
2 portions
Allergens: G

Quantity of ingredients
Cottage cheese 3/4 lbs / 300g. (yes)
Apple (sour) 1 piece / 100g. (little)
Pear 1 piece / 100g. (yes)

Cooking instructions:
Wash apples and pears well, do not peel, and chop small. In a pot with steam filter, boil them al dente, remove and allow to cool down.
Serve the cheese, spread the fruit on it.

9.32 Couscous Salad

prevents cancer, forcing spleen, promotes digestion, stimulates liver function, reduces blood pressure, strengthens immune system, reduces radiation damage, diuretic.
Cooking time approx. 25 min
Calories p. portion: 338
3 portions
Allergens: A

Quantity of ingredients
Couscous 5/8 oz / 200g. (yes)
Water 1 cup / 100g. (yes)
Chives 1 Bunch / 100g. (yes)
Olive oil 1 table spoon / 15g. (yes)
Parsley 1 Bunch / 100g. (yes)
Peppermint 3 twigs / 30g. (yes)
Lemon juice 2 table spoons / 30g. (yes)
Lemon peel 1 teaspoon / 2g. (yes)
Tomato 2 pieces / 80g. (yes)
Cucumber 1/4 lbs - 4oz / 100g. (yes)
Carrot 1/4 lbs - 4oz / 100g. (yes)

Cooking instructions:
Boil in a small saucepan 250 ml. water with salt and 1 tablespoon olive oil. Add the couscous, take the stove in the front and let it swell covered for 5 minutes. Put the couscous back on the stove and let it simmer for about 2 minutes with gentle stirring. If necessary, add 1 - 3 tbsp of hot water.
Mix the couscous with lemon juice, chopped lemon peel and 1 tbsp oil, season with salt and pepper and leave to set.
Add couscous with tomatoes, cucumber, parsley (all diced), carrots (grated), chives and mint (finely chopped).
Season the couscous salad with lemon juice, salt and pepper.

9.33 Cranberry yogurt mix

Good to fight acute or chronic constipation of the intestine, oral mucosal inflammation, diarrhea, flatulence, throat irritation.
Cooking time approx. 5 min
Calories p. portion: 57
2 portions
Allergens: GO

Quantity of ingredients
Mineral water 1 cup / 250g. (little)
Cranberry jam 2 table spoons / 20g. (yes)
Yogurt (natural, 1.5% fat) 1/4 lbs - 4oz / 125g. (yes)

Cooking instructions:
Mix yoghurt, cranberry jam and mineral water until frothy.

9.34 Cream cheese substitute

Good to fight lactose intolerance. Strengthens body energy, promotes digestion, promotes weight loss. Good to fight immunodeficiency, loss of appetite, arteriosclerosis, flatulence, bladder weakness, anemia.
Cooking time approx. 20 min
Calories p. portion: 526
2 portions
Allergens: AE

Quantity of ingredients
Herbs various 2 table spoons / 6g. (yes)
Whole grain bread 6 slices / 300g. (recommended)
Soybean milk 4 cup / 300g. (yes)
Lemon 1 piece / 50g. (yes)

Cooking instructions:
Heat the soy milk in a saucepan till it boils, stirring occasionally (gets burn easily!), Then allow to cool.
Squeeze out the lemon and stir gently under the cooled soy milk (approx. 80°C/176°F), let it approx. 20 min. rest or clot.
Pour chopped soy milk through a strainer lined with a dishcloth, allow liquid to drain and then squeeze out
remaining liquid with the dishcloth.
Refine to taste with fresh herbs.
Serve with wholemeal bread.

9.35 Cucumber soup

Diuretic, detoxifying, suppresses conversion of sugar into fat, lowers cholesterol, prevents cancer, promotes digestion, diaphoretic, dries out, good to fight yeast infections.
Cooking time approx. 20 min
Calories p. portion: 96
4 portions
Allergens: M

Quantity of ingredients
Cucumber 2 pieces / 400g. (yes)
Coriander 1 pinch / 1g. (yes)
Cardamom 1 pinch / 1g. (yes)
Olive oil 2 table spoons / 35g. (yes)
Salt 1 pinch / 1g. (little)
Sage 3 leaves / 3g. (yes)
Water 2 cup / 500g. (yes)
Mustard 1/2 teaspoon / 0,5g. (yes)

Cooking instructions:
Heat oil and roast short the small cucumbers. Add Mustard seeds, coriander, cardamom and salt. Add water.
Simmer for 10-15 min. Puree and decorate with fresh chopped sage.

9.36 Delicately spiced zucchini with tomatoes

Diuretic, promotes digestion, helps to digest fat, reduces blood pressure, dissolves stagnation, antioxidative, supports urination, diuretic, warming the body from the inside, expands blood vessels.
Cooking time approx. 10 min
Calories p. portion: 203
4 portions
Allergens: -

Quantity of ingredients
Tomato 2 pieces / 120g. (yes)
Salt 1 pinch / 1g. (little)
Basil (fresh) 6-8 leaves / 3g. (yes)
Salt 1 pinch / 1g. (little)
Water 6 cups / 400g. (yes)
Rice (whole grain) 1 cup / 120g. (recommended)
Onion white 2 pieces / 120g. (yes)
Zucchini 4 pieces / 800g. (recommended)
Olive oil 1 table spoon / 20g. (yes)
Oregano dried 1 pinch / 1g. (yes)

Cooking instructions:
In a hot pan, fry olive oil, finely chopped onions and finely chopped zucchini until half cooked. Add plenty of dried oregano. Salt and chop the tomatoes for a few minutes until the zucchini are tender but crisp. Add fresh basil as desired. Variation: Put some sheep's cheese over the tomatoes and finish cooking with the lid closed. Place the rice in salted

water, heat till it boils and let it simmer over low heat for about 15 minutes.

9.37 Exotic lenses

Strengthens heart and kidney, diuretic, dalms the stomach, promotes digestion, dissolves stagnation, helps to digest fat, supports urination, reduces blood pressure, detoxifying and stimulating the immune system.
Cooking time approx. 45 min
Calories p. portion: 144
4 portions
Allergens: NO

Quantity of ingredients
Rice (whole grain) 1/2 cup / 60g. (recommended)
Sesame oil 1 table spoon / 10g. (little)
Salt 1 pinch / 1g. (little)
Salt 1 pinch / 1g. (little)
Chard 5/8 oz / 200g. (recommended)
Lentils red 1 cup / 120g. (recommended)
Lemon 1/2 piece / 20g. (yes)
Cauliflower 5/8 oz / 200g. (recommended)
Tomato 1 piece / 50g. (yes)
Thyme dried 1/2 teaspoon / 1g. (yes)
Bocksdorn fruits (Fructus Lycii, goji berry dried 2 pinches / 2g. (yes)
Cumin (Caraway seed) 1/2 teaspoon / 2g. (yes)
Wakame 1 inch / 1g. (yes)
Ginger fresh 1/2 teaspoon / 2g. (yes)
Sugar cane sugar 1 pinch / 1g. (little)
Onion white 2 pieces / 120g. (yes)
Salt 1 pinch / 1g. (little)
Water 3 cups / 300g. (yes)
Vinegar (Apple vinegar) 1/2 teaspoon / 1g. (yes)

Cooking instructions:
Heat sesame oil in a hot pot. Add chopped onions, grated ginger, dried thyme, plenty of cumin and sauté gently.
Add peeled red lentils, a strip of wakame, a little lemon juice, hot water and some dried buckthorn fruits. Simmer for 20 minutes until the lentils are cooked; add hot water as needed to make a pulp. Add sugar, some chili and salt.
Add vinegar or lemon juice depending on your taste. Add chopped

tomatoes as desired. Let it pass for a few minutes.
Cook in a small pot with 1 cup of water and a little salt the cauliflower 10 min. until soft.
Blanch in a small pot with 1 cup of water and salt the chard 3 min.
Boil the rice briefly, salt and 10 min. to let go. Serve everything with the lentil dish.

9.38 Fennel and potato gratin

Reduces inflammation, improves blood circulation, improves digestion, supports urination, lowers cholesterol, good to fight loss of appetite, flatulence, inflammatory bowel disease, heartburn. Forcing spleen, improves blood
Cooking time approx. 1 1/2 hours
Calories p. portion: 147
2 portions
Allergens: CGL

Quantity of ingredients
Basic recipe for a vegetable soup (nutritious) 1/2 cup / 100g. (yes)
Potato 1/4 lbs - 4oz / 125g. (yes)
Butter Bio 1 teaspoon / 3g. (little)
Salt 1 pinch / 1g. (little)
Chicken yolk 1 piece / 10g. (little)
Pepper Cayenne 1 pinch / 0,5g. (yes)
Cream sour 10% 1 teaspoon / 3g. (yes)
Fennel 5/8 oz / 200g. (yes)
Rice flour 2 teaspoons / 6g. (little)
Parsley 1 teaspoon / 2g. (yes)
Chives 1 teaspoon / 3g. (yes)
Butter Bio 1 teaspoon / 3g. (little)
Parmesan 1 teaspoon / 3g. (yes)
Nutmeg 1 pinch / 0,5g. (yes)
Sugar cane sugar 1 pinch / 1g. (little)

Cooking instructions:
Cook peeled potatoes and then let cool. Wash the fennel, cut off the stems and remove any outer leaves.
Hold back fennel greens and add it to the sauce with the other herbs later.
Steam the fennel tubers for about 15 - 20 minutes.
Then cut the potatoes and fennel into slices and place in layers in a greased baking dish. Bring the liquid of fennel broth to the boil and bind

it with flour.
Season with sea salt, cayenne pepper, sugar, nutmeg and sour cream. Allow to cool and alloy with egg yolk.
Spread the sauce over the casserole, sprinkle with parmesan and finely chopped parsley and chives. Bake at 200 ° C in the oven for half an hour.

9.39 Fennel with roasted walnuts

Forcing spleen, detoxifying, reduces inflammation, improves blood circulation, improves medication effect, stimulates appetite, antioxidativ, promotes digestion, stimulates, dissolves stagnation.
Cooking time approx. 20 min
Calories p. portion: 342
4 portions
Allergens: HO

Quantity of ingredients
Corn Grease (Polenta) 1 cup / 120g. (yes)
Walnuts 2 table spoons / 35g. (yes)
Nutmeg 1 pinch / 1g. (yes)
White wine 1/2 cup / 125g. (little)
Ginger fresh 1/2 teaspoon / 1g. (yes)
Salt 1 pinch / 1g. (little)
Olive oil 2 table spoons / 40g. (yes)
Water 1 1/2 cups / 220g. (yes)
Salt 1 pinch / 1g. (little)
Peppers powder 1 pinch / 1g. (yes)
Fennel 4 pieces / 800g. (yes)

Cooking instructions:
Heat very little water in a pot; Fry the fennel in strips. Add Nutmeg, a little grated ginger, add salt, a dash of white wine, rose paprika.
Simmer until the vegetables are cooked, but still crisp; stir in a little olive oil; sprinkle with roasted walnuts.
Stir the polenta into a pot of hot water, stirring constantly, until the polenta has the desired consistency. Salt.
Pull the polenta off the fire and let it swell for about 10 minutes.

9.40 Figs with mozzarella and honey

Promotes digestion, reduces inflammation, bloating and nausea, relaxing and reassuring, relieves pain, detoxifying, blood stilling, forcing spleen and digestive system, detoxifying, bactericide.

Cooking time approx. 10 min
Calories p. portion: 415
1 portions
Allergens: GO

Quantity of ingredients
Grapeseed oil 1 table spoon / 12g. (little)
Basil (fresh) 1/2 bunch / 50g. (yes)
Vinegar Aceto Balsamico white 1 table spoon / 12g. (yes)
Fig 4 pieces / 100g. (recommended)
Honey 2 table spoons / 24g. (little)
Mozzarella 1 piece / 50g. (yes)
Pepper (ground) 1 pinch / 0,1g. (yes)

Cooking instructions:
Quarter fresh figs, dice buffalo mozzarella, pluck basil leaves.
Mix a dressing with light balsamic vinegar, grapeseed oil and honey and season to taste.
Place the figs on the edge of the appropriate plate. Spread the mozzarella cubes and season with black pepper.
Spread whole or roughly sliced basil leaves over it and moisten with the marinade. Spiced pizza bread goes perfectly with it.

9.41 Fish soup with rosemary

Promotes spleen and liver, reduces blood pressure, strengthens immune system, prevents cancer, reduces radiation damage, has little cholesterol and is protein rich, improves blood circulation, increases appetite. Antioxidant, forcing spleen, dissolves stagnation.
Cooking time approx. 30 min
Calories p. portion: 271
4 portions
Allergens: DLO

Quantity of ingredients
Peppercorns 2 pieces / 1g. (yes)
Celery root 1 slice / 20g. (yes)
Onion (spring onion) 1 piece / 20g. (yes)
Olive oil 2 table spoons / 35g. (yes)
Basic recipe for a fish soup 2 cup / 500g. (yes)
Salt 1 pinch / 1g. (little)
Rosemary 1/2 bunch / 7g. (yes)
Carrot 1 piece / 120g. (yes)

Fish pieces mixed (fresh water) 5/8 lbs - 8oz / 250g. (yes)
Garlic 1 clove / 3g. (yes)
Parsnip 1 piece / 180g. (yes)

Cooking instructions:
Fry the onion and garlic in oil. Add fish broth. Add diced carrots, parsnips and celery. Season with salt and peppercorns. Simmer the soup on a low heat for 25 minutes.
Wash the fish, drizzle with lemon juice, divide into pieces and add to the soup with the pink rosemary. Cook for 5 min on low heat.
Add the chives and parsley and season the soup with the salt.

9.42 Fried apple

Good to fight acute or chronic constipation of the intestine, warming stomach and spleen, improves blood circulation. Good to fight kidney weakness, back pain and abdominal pain, impotence.
Cooking time approx. 30 min
Calories p. portion: 408
4 portions
Allergens: GH

Quantity of ingredients
Apple (sour) 4 pieces / 500g. (little)
Yoghurt vanilla 3 cups / 750g. (yes)
Cinnamon ground 1 pinch / 1g. (yes)
Sugar - icing sugar 2 table spoons / 36g. (little)
Almond 1/8 lbs - 2oz / 50g. (yes)
Vanilla sugar natural 1 package / 3g. (little)
Cow's milk (whole milk 3.5% fat) 2 table spoons / 24g. (yes)
Cinnamon ground 1 pinch / 0,2g. (yes)
Hazelnuts 1/8 lbs - 2oz / 50g. (yes)

Cooking instructions:
Wash the apples, cut off a lid, cut out the core casing with a teaspoon so that the apple remains a tight bottom.
Mix nuts, almonds, fructose, milk, vanilla sugar, cinnamon well. Fill into the apples. Put the covers back on.
Bake in preheated oven at 180 ° C for approx. 20 minutes.
Mix icing sugar and cinnamon.
Spread vanilla yoghurt on plate, place 1 baked apple on each, sprinkle with cinnamon-powdered sugar mixture.
Serve hot immediately!

9.43 Frozen pineapple juice

Pineapple reduce inflammation, supports urination, cleans the skin.
Cooking time approx. 1 1/2 hours
Calories p. portion: 29
1 portions
Allergens: -

Quantity of ingredients
Pineapple 1/8 lbs - 2oz / 50g. (yes)

Cooking instructions:
Juice pineapple yourself or freeze the organic pineapple juice in small portions and if necessary suck.

9.44 Fruit juice

Stops diarrhea, promotes digestion, appetizing, harmonizes the stomach, relieves pain, detoxifying, reduces blood pressure, strengthens immune system, prevents cancer, reduces radiation damage.
Cooking time approx. 10 min
Calories p. portion: 176
2 portions
Allergens: -

Quantity of ingredients
Orange 2 pieces / 150g. (yes)
Carrot 2 pieces / 150g. (yes)
Honey 1 table spoon / 10g. (little)
Apple (sweet) 4 pieces / 300g. (little)

Cooking instructions:
Peel oranges and carrots. Cut all ingredients into cubes so that they fit into the juicer and juice. Sweet with honey.

9.45 Grapefruit juice

Promotes digestion, lowers blood glucose, dries out, provides Vitamin C
Cooking time approx. 5 min
Calories p. portion: 107
1 portions
Allergens: -

Quantity of ingredients
Grapefruit (Pomelo) 1 cup / 250g. (yes)

Cooking instructions:
Juice fresh grapefruit or use organic juice.

9.46 Halibut with tomato and garlic sauce

Promotes digestion, helps to digest fat, supports urination, reduces blood pressure, good to fight rheumatism, flatulence, bladder weakness, anemia, high blood pressure, depressions, diabetes, diarrhea. Valuable omega-3 fatty acids.
Cooking time approx. 45 min
Calories p. portion: 319
5 portions
Allergens: D

Quantity of ingredients
Rice variety any 1 cup / 120g. (little)
Garlic 8 pieces / 10g. (yes)
Thyme dried 1 table spoon / 5g. (yes)
Olives 0,2 lbs / 75g. (yes)
Tomato 4 pieces / 200g. (yes)
Salt 1 pinch / 1g. (little)
Lemon 1 piece / 30g. (yes)
Bay leaf 2 pieces / 2g. (yes)
Water 6 cups / 240g. (yes)
Salt 1 pinch / 1g. (little)
Halibut (Flatfish) 2,2 lbs / 800g. (yes)
Salt 1 pinch / 1g. (little)
Lemon juice 1 dach / 2g. (yes)
Pepper (ground) 1 pinch / 0,5g. (yes)
Pepper (ground) 1 pinch / 0,5g. (yes)

Cooking instructions:
Cook rice with salted water (1:3).
Rinse the fish under running cold water, dab with kitchen paper and rub with salt, pepper and lemon juice.
Place the fish fillets in a casserole dish with pieces of bay leaf.
Wash the lemon hot and cut into slices, peel and halve the garlic.
Sprinkle the olives and the thyme over them.
Brew the tomatoes with hot water, skin and chop.
Mix all ingredients, season with salt and pepper and distribute around

the fish.
Cook everything at 200°C/392°F for about 20 minutes.
Serve with the rice.

9.47 Hearty polenta mash

Strengths spleen and stomach, promotes watering, promotes digestion, detoxifying, promotes perspiration, reduces blood lipids, stimulates, dissolves stagnation, stimulates appetite, dissolves stagnation.
Cooking time approx. 10 min
Calories p. portion: 262
2 portions
Allergens: -

Quantity of ingredients
Water 1 1/2 cups / 240g. (yes)
Onion (spring onion) 2 pieces / 40g. (yes)
Corn Grease (Polenta) 1 cup / 120g. (yes)
Nutmeg 1 pinch / 1g. (yes)
Olive oil 1 table spoon / 10g. (yes)
Salt 1 pinch / 1g. (little)
Ginger fresh 1/2 teaspoon / 2g. (yes)
Turmeric (yellow root) 1 pinch / 1g. (yes)

Cooking instructions:
Stir in the polenta in boiling water and let it swell for 7 min. Add green onion, grated ginger, turmeric, nutmeg, salt and olive oil and wait for 3 more minutes.

9.48 Hearty winter breakfast

Strengthens immune system, calms nerves and stomach, promotes digestion, detoxifying, strengthens bodily production, promotes perspiration, reduces blood lipids, stimulates, dissolves stagnation.
Cooking time approx. 20 min
Calories p. portion: 678
1 portions
Allergens: ACEG

Quantity of ingredients
Chicken egg 1 piece / 55g. (little)
Onion (spring onion) 2 pieces / 40g. (yes)
Ginger fresh 1/2 teaspoon / 1g. (yes)
Salt 1 pinch / 1g. (little)

Oat meal 1 cup / 120g. (recommended)
Butter Bio 1 table spoon / 15g. (little)
Soy sauce 1 dash / 3g. (yes)

Cooking instructions:
Soak oatmeal overnight. Boil in the morning with a little ginger, salt and a spring onion or leek and then let it swell until the porridge is soft. Before serving, add a whole egg to the porridge, add the butter and season to taste with a little soy sauce.
Recommendation: Especially suitable for the cold season.

9.49 Hot water with grape juice

Calms stomach, strengthens tendons and bones, supports urination, promotes digestion.
Cooking time approx. 5 min
Calories p. portion: 87
1 portions
Allergens: -

Quantity of ingredients
Grape juice red 1 cup / 120g. (yes)
Water 1/2 cup / 60g. (yes)

Cooking instructions:
Heat the water till it boils and add it to the grape juice.

9.50 Lasagne with tofu cream

Harmonizes spleen and stomach, reduces Flatulence, protects the digestive system. Good to fight lack of appetite, flatulence, inflammatory bowel disease, stomach ulcers, rheumatism, heartburn, twelffinger intestinal
Cooking time approx. 45 min
Calories p. portion: 301
4 portions
Allergens: ACEG

Quantity of ingredients
Edam cheese 1/8 lbs - 2oz / 50g. (yes)
Peppers powder 1 pinch / 1g. (yes)
Marjoram 1 pinch / 1g. (yes)
Tomato 1/4 lbs - 4oz / 100g. (yes)
Oregano dried 1 pinch / 1g. (yes)

Salt 1 pinch / 1g. (little)
Noodles (wheat, lasagne) with egg 3/8 lbs - 6oz / 150g. (little)
Soy Tofu 7/8 lbs / 400g. (yes)
Chicken egg 2 pieces / 100g. (little)
Onion white 2 pieces / 120g. (yes)

Cooking instructions:
Tofu cream: Mix tofu with eggs, onions, small tomatoes, oregano, marjoram, peppers and some sea salt put into a smooth mass using a kitchen machine with a knife or a blender.
Lasagne: Place 1/5 of the tofu cream in a casserole dish (25x15cm), cover with 3 lasagna leaves, repeat this process twice, and then finish the last fifth of the tofu cream over the pastry plates. Sprinkle with a little grated Edam and bake in the oven at 175°C/347°F for about 1/2 hour.

9.51 Lettuce with fresh cheese

The bitter substances have diuretic effect and promote the blood circulation in the digestive area. Mustard improves thyroid function, relieves rheumatism symptoms.
Cooking time approx. 5 min
Calories p. portion: 802
1 portions
Allergens: AFM

Quantity of ingredients
Herbs various 2 teaspoons / 4g. (yes)
Fresh cheese from soya 3/8 lbs - 6oz / 150g. (yes)
Leaf salads (bitter) 2 portions / 60g. (yes)
Black caraway 1 pinch / 1g. (yes)
Pepper (ground) 1 pinch / 0,5g. (yes)
Mustard 1 knife tip / 1g. (yes)
Lemon juice 1 dash / 3g. (yes)
Salt 1 pinch / 1g. (little)
Whole grain bread 2 slices / 40g. (recommended)

Cooking instructions:
Wash lettuce and finely pluck.
Mix 150 ml cream cheese, splashes of mustard, splashes of lemon juice, 1 clove of garlic, chopped fresh herbs,
pinch of pepper and crushed black cumin and pour over. Serve with wholemeal bread.

9.52 Lettuce with vinegar dressing

Relieves fatigue, regulates gastrointestinal function, dissolves stagnation, laxative, antiparasitic, improves blood circulation, detoxifying, reduces inflammation, relieves pain.
Cooking time approx. 10 min
Calories p. portion: 68
2 portions
Allergens: O

Quantity of ingredients
Vinegar (Apple vinegar) 1 table spoon / 10g. (yes)
Lettuce 1 piece / 200g. (yes)
Rapeseed oil 1 table spoon / 10g. (yes)
Onion (spring onion) 1 piece / 20g. (yes)
Pepper (ground) 1 pinch / 0,1g. (yes)
Salt 1 pinch / 0,5g. (little)
Water 1 table spoon / 10g. (yes)
Chives 1 table spoon / 5g. (yes)

Cooking instructions:
Clean lettuce, wash and drain. Add the ingredients to the marinade in an extra container. Salad with marinade just before consumption. Just before, sprinkle with chives.

9.53 Marinated cod on pumpkin puree

Reduces inflammation, improves digestion, promotes spleen, lung, stomach and kidneys, diuretic, reduces blood glucose, good to fight constipation and flatulence, dissolves stagnation.
Cooking time approx. 2 hours
Calories p. portion: 202
4 portions
Allergens: DG

Quantity of ingredients
Olive oil 1 teaspoon / 3g. (yes)
Pepper (ground) 1 pinch / 0,3g. (yes)
Oregano dried 1/4 teaspoon / 1g. (yes)
Salt 1 pinch / 1g. (little)
Salt 1 pinch / 1g. (little)
Lemon juice 1/2 piece / 15g. (yes)
Basil (fresh) 1/2 teaspoon / 2g. (yes)
Pumpkin 5/8 oz / 200g. (yes)

Oregano dried 1/2 teaspoon / 1g. (yes)
Onion white 1 piece / 50g. (yes)
Potato 6 pieces / 400g. (yes)
Pepper (ground) 1 pinch / 0,3g. (yes)
Cod 3/4 lbs / 300g. (yes)
Yogurt (natural, 1.5% fat) 3/8 lbs - 6oz / 150g. (yes)
Crème fraiche cheese 2 table spoons / 30g. (little)

Cooking instructions:
Mix yoghurt with oregano, basil and thyme.
Wash the fish fillets, pat dry, place in a flat shape and pour over the marinade. Leave 2 hours in refrigerator.
Cook the potatoes in salted water until soft and peel.
Sauté the onion in oil until glassy, add the diced pumpkin and cook for about 10 min. Add oregano, lemon juice, salt, pepper and creme fraiche and puree with the blender.
Remove fish fillets from the marinade, drain, pat dry and salt. Coat a coated grill pan with 2 teaspoons of oil. Roast the fish fillets on both sides for 3 - 4 minutes and arrange with the potatoes on the pumpkin puree.

9.54 Millet with pears

Refreshing and nourishing, promotes digestion, supports urination, reduces blood lipids, stimulates, dissolves stagnation, forces liver, strengthens the muscles, lowers cholesterol.
Cooking time approx. 35 min
Calories p. portion: 213
5 portions
Allergens: G

Quantity of ingredients
Acerola fruit nectar or powder 1 teaspoon / 2g. (little)
Salt 1 pinch / 1g. (little)
Barley malt 1/2 teaspoon / 2g. (yes)
Ginger fresh 1/2 teaspoon / 2g. (yes)
Sunflower seeds 2 table spoons / 4g. (recommended)
Pear 4 pieces / 600g. (yes)
Cocoa 1 pinch / 1g. (yes)
Millet 1 cup / 120g. (recommended)
Grape juice red 1 1/2 cups / 240g. (yes)
Water 1 1/2 cups / 200g. (yes)
Cream, sweet 30% 2 teaspoons / 20g. (little)

Cooking instructions:
Simmer the millet for 5 min and let it swell for another 30 min.

Then: In a hot pot, heat some grape juice; add chopped pears, very little grated ginger, a pinch of salt, acerola, a pinch of cocoa and sauté briefly; add the boiled millet, sunflower seeds, some barley malt to taste, 1 tsp cream per serving or a little butter.

9.55 Millet with shiitake mushrooms and avocado

Anti-inflammatory, good to fight swelling and pain, promotes spleen and kidney, diuretic, stimulates digestion, building up, eye-enhancing, detoxifying, nerve-strengthening, building up.
Cooking time approx. 20 min
Calories p. portion: 560
2 portions
Allergens: G

Quantity of ingredients
Water 1 1/2 cups / 200g. (yes)
Rucola 2 handful / 30g. (yes)
Millet 1 cup / 120g. (recommended)
Ginger fresh 1/2 teaspoon / 2g. (yes)
Pepper (ground) 1 pinch / 0,5g. (yes)
Shiitake, dried 1 oz / 25g. (yes)
Lemon juice 1 dash / 3g. (yes)
Parsley 1 table spoon / 7g. (yes)
Avocado 1 piece / 200g. (yes)
Salt 1 pinch / 1g. (little)
Butter Bio 1 table spoon / 15g. (little)
Peppers powder 1 pinch / 1g. (yes)

Cooking instructions:
In a saucepan with hot water, sprinkle the millet, add in strips cut shiitake mushrooms and some ginger and simmer; add a pinch of ground pepper, a little salt, plenty of parsley, a pinch of rose pepper, stir in a piece of butter.
In the meantime: place ½ peeled avocado per serving on one half of the plate: sprinkle with a little ground pepper, a small pinch of salt; drizzle with lemon juice; sprinkle a little chopped rocket or rose paprika over it. Put the millet dish on the other half of the plate.

9.56 Miso soup with tofu

Vitamins, minerals and secondary plant active ingredients, invigorating, detoxifying, strengthens immune system, promotes digestion, forcing spleen, containing enzymes, reduces flatulence, alginic acid detoxifies the bowel, dissolves stagnation.
Cooking time approx. 5 min
Calories p. portion: 51
3 portions
Allergens: E

Quantity of ingredients
Soy Tofu 1/8 lbs - 2oz / 50g. (yes)
Soy sauce 1 dash / 3g. (yes)
Water 2 cup / 500g. (yes)
Wakame 1 piece / 5g. (yes)
Onion (spring onion) 1/2 teaspoon / 6g. (yes)
Miso 3-4 table spoons / 30g. (yes)

Cooking instructions:
Boil soybean seedlings, wakame algae and diced tofu for 5 minutes. Put the miso paste in the soup plate and slowly pour over the soup. Season with Tamari sauce. Sprinkle with cutted spring onion.

9.57 Nettle-chard soup

Nettle promotes urination, detoxifies, supporting prostate disorders, reduces inflammation, analgesic. Chard supports intestinal activity, cleans intestine.
Cooking time approx. 30 min
Calories p. portion: 52
4 portions
Allergens: -

Quantity of ingredients
Olive oil 1 table spoon / 10g. (yes)
Pepper (ground) 1 pinch / 0,5g. (yes)
Nettles Handful / 10g. (yes)
Chard 1 lbs / 500g. (recommended)
Water 2 cup / 400g. (yes)
Salt 1 pinch / 1g. (little)

Cooking instructions:
Heat the oil in a saucepan, add the washed and finely chopped Swiss

chard. Salt and let simmer for 10 minutes.
Add the chopped nettles and cook for another 10 minutes. Add pepper and puree.

9.58 Noodle casserole with plugs and peaches

Relieves fatigue, relaxes, good tro fight belching, acute or chronic obstruction of the bowel, flatulence, heartburn. Calms nerves and stomach, strengthens the defense, good to fight fungi infections.
Cooking time approx. 1 hour
Calories p. portion: 442
4 portions
Allergens: ACGO

Quantity of ingredients
Cinnamon ground 1/4 teaspoon / 1g. (yes)
Strawberry jam 4 table spoons / 50g. (little)
Curd cheese 20% 5/8 lbs - 8oz / 250g. (yes)
Butter Bio 2 teaspoons / 8g. (little)
Chicken egg 2 pieces / 120g. (little)
Noodles (wheat, ribbon noodles) with egg 5/8 oz / 200g. (little)
Peaches 1,1 lbs / 500g. (yes)
Lemon peel 1/2 piece / 2g. (yes)
Vanilla sugar natural 3 package / 3g. (little)
Sugar - icing sugar 1/8 lbs - 2oz / 40g. (little)

Cooking instructions:
Preheat oven to 180°C/356°F.
Put Peaches briefly in boiling water, drain and peel off the skin. Cut peaches into small slices.
Cook noodles in plenty of salted water until firm, drain, chill off cold and drain.
Separate eggs. Stir egg yolks with icing sugar, vanilla sugar, grated lemon zest and cinnamon until fluffy with the whisk. Stir in the curd cheese. Add the noodles.
Beat the egg whites into firm snow and carefully lift them under the pasta.
Spread a baking dish thinly with butter. Alternating pate noodle mixture and peach slices into the form layers. Finish with the pasta mixture.
Sprinkle the casserole with butter flakes and bake in a preheated oven for 3o minutes.
Serve portion by portion with a tablespoon of jam.

9.59 Oat flakes with aromatic spices

Stops diarrhea, promotes digestion, appetizing, harmonizes the stomach, relieves diarrhea, strengthens immune system, detoxifying and stimulating the immune system.
Cooking time approx. 25 min
Calories p. portion: 280
3 portions
Allergens: AH

Quantity of ingredients
Walnuts 1 table spoon / 15g. (yes)
Hazelnuts 1 table spoon / 15g. (yes)
Apple (sweet) 1 piece / 220g. (little)
Water 1 1/2 cups / 240g. (yes)
Lemon Balm (fresh) 3-4 leaves / 3g. (yes)
Cardamom 3-4 capsules / 2g. (yes)
Wakame 1 inch / 2g. (yes)
Acerola fruit nectar or powder 1 teaspoon / 2g. (little)
Oat flakes (whole grain) 1 cup / 125g. (recommended)

Cooking instructions:
Roast oatmeal and nuts. Add hot water. Add cardamom, wakame and cook for 20 min. Add grated apple, acerola and lemon herb.

9.60 Oatmeal soup with spring onion and carrots

Reduces blood pressure, strengthens immune system, prevents cancer, reduces radiation damage, stimulates digestion, reduces pain, stimulates appetite, dissolves stagnation.
Cooking time approx. 30 min
Calories p. portion: 135
3 portions
Allergens: AG

Quantity of ingredients
Onion (spring onion) 2 pieces / 40g. (yes)
Carrot 2 pieces / 200g. (yes)
Oat 6 table spoons / 48g. (recommended)
Butter Bio 1 table spoon / 15g. (little)
Nutmeg 1 pinch / 1g. (yes)
Lovage 1 stem / 15g. (yes)
Water 2 cup / 480g. (yes)

Cooking instructions:
Roast the oats in butter, add salt and spices, pour in water and heat till it boils. After 10 min. add the grated carrots and lovage, cook for 10 minutes. Finely add chopped onion.

9.61 Olive oil with lemon juice

Good to fight acute constipation.
Cooking time approx. 1 min
Calories p. portion: 93
1 portions
Allergens: -

Quantity of ingredients
Olive oil 1 table spoon / 10g. (yes)
Lemon juice 1 teaspoon / 4g. (yes)

Cooking instructions:
In case of acute constipation take 1 tablespoon of olive oil with lemon juice in the morning on an empty stomach.

9.62 Oven potatoes with celery-curd cheese (quark)

Promotes spleen, reduces Inflammation, improves digestion, regenerates skin, supports urination, lowers cholesterol.
Cooking time approx. 30 min
Calories p. portion: 304
2 portions
Allergens: GL

Quantity of ingredients
Potato 6 pieces / 400g. (yes)
Ground caraway 1 pinch / 0,2g. (yes)
Lemon peel 1/2 teaspoon / 1g. (yes)
Salt 1 pinch / 1g. (little)
Pepper (ground) 1 pinch / 0,2g. (yes)
Lemon juice 1 teaspoon / 3g. (yes)
Basic recipe for a vegetable soup (nutritious) 1/2 cup / 100g. (yes)
Creme fraiche cheese 1/2 teaspoon / 5g. (little)
Celery root 3 oz / 80g. (yes)
Olive oil 2 teaspoons / 5g. (yes)
Salt 1 pinch / 1g. (little)
Curd cheese 20% 5/8 oz / 200g. (yes)

Cooking instructions:
Celery-curd cheese:
Mix celery with vegetable broth according to basic recipe, caraway and lemon peel. Cook for about 8 minutes until the celery is soft and the vegetable broth almost evaporated. Mix the celery vegetable broth with the lemon juice, finely, and stir until smooth. Season with salt and pepper.

Baked potatoes:
Preheat oven to 200 °C / 400 °F.
Brush the potatoes well, halve them, and place them on a baking tray with the cut surface facing up. Lightly salt the surfaces and sprinkle with oil. Fry the potatoes in the oven for about 25 minutes.
Serve the celery plug to the potatoes.

9.63 Oyster mushrooms with asparagus

Forces, reduces inflammation, improves digestion, lowers cholesterol, strengthens kidney, stimulates liver function, improves blood circulation, improves medication effect, increases appetite.
Cooking time approx. 30 min
Calories p. portion: 316
4 portions
Allergens: GH

Quantity of ingredients
Salt 1 pinch / 1g. (little)
Potato 1 lbs / 500g. (yes)
Sake 2 table spoons / 40g. (yes)
Salt (herbal) 1 pinch / 1g. (little)
Oyster mushroom 3/4 lbs / 300g. (yes)
Butter Bio 2 table spoons / 40g. (little)
Onion white 1 piece / 50g. (yes)
Sugar white 1 pinch / 0,1g. (little)
Asparagus (green or white) 1,1 lbs / 500g. (yes)
Parsley 2 table spoons / 40g. (yes)
Walnuts 2 table spoons / 60g. (yes)

Cooking instructions:
Cook organically grown potatoes with the skin, otherwise prepare peeled boiled potatoes. Boil the asparagus in salted water with a pinch of sugar and salt. (You can cook an old roll that absorbs the bittering substances.) Slightly sauté the chopped onions in a pan in the butter

before frying the oyster mushrooms cut into the same pan.
Stew 15 minutes, stirring several times. Add the sake, walnuts and parsley and simmer on low heat while you drain the potatoes and asparagus. Finally, sprinkle some herbal salt over it.
If no fresh asparagus is available, asparagus can be used in jars.

9.64 Pancakes with spinach and parmesan

Promotes bowel movement, strengthens immune system, good to fight loss of appetite, flatulence, high blood pressure, depressions, diabetes, constipation, inflammatory bowel disease
Cooking time approx. 25 min
Calories p. portion: 330
6 portions
Allergens: ACGL

Quantity of ingredients
Basil (fresh) 1/4 teaspoon / 1g. (yes)
Nutmeg 1 pinch / 0,3g. (yes)
Crème fraiche cheese 2 table spoons / 45g. (little)
Spinach 1,3 lbs / 600g. (yes)
Parmesan 1/8 lbs - 2oz / 60g. (yes)
Salt 1 pinch / 1g. (little)
Salt 1 pinch / 1g. (little)
Basic recipe for a vegetable soup (nutritious) 1/2 cup / 150g. (yes)
Pepper (ground) 1 pinch / 0,1g. (yes)
Onion white 1 piece / 50g. (yes)
Sunflower oil 1 table spoon / 15g. (little)
Cow's milk (whole milk 3.5% fat) 1 1/2 cups / 400g. (yes)
Chicken egg 4 pieces / 200g. (little)
Wheat flour 1/4 lbs - 4oz / 100g. (yes)
Wholemeal flour 1/4 lbs - 4oz / 100g. (recommended)
Olive oil 1 table spoon / 15g. (yes)
Parsley 1/2 bunch / 80g. (yes)

Cooking instructions:
Stir flour, eggs and milk and a pinch of salt with the whisk until smooth. From the dough, fry pancakes crispy brown on both sides.
Heat oil in a small saucepan. Fry the finely chopped onion until tender. Stir in chopped parsley, sauté briefly. Add the vegetable broth according to the basic recipe, season with basil and nutmeg. Cover and simmer for 15 minutes, add crème fraiche and finely puree.
Cook the washed, drizzled spinach with a little salt in a closed pan over

a moderate heat in 3 minutes, drain in a sieve and cut into small pieces. Add the spinach to the sauce, heat briefly. Add parmesan in the mix. Fill the pancakes with the cream spinach.

9.65 Pear compote

Promotes digestion, supports urination.
Cooking time approx. 20 min
Calories p. portion: 100
3 portions
Allergens: -

Quantity of ingredients
Water 1 1/2 cups / 240g. (yes)
Pear 4 / 500g. (yes)

Cooking instructions:
Halve organic pears. Cores and skin can be used. Pear in the pot and add water. Simmer for up to 20 minutes until pears are tender.

9.66 Pear juice

Promotes digestion, supports urination.
Cooking time approx. 5 min
Calories p. portion: 180
2 portions
Allergens: -

Quantity of ingredients
Pear 3 pieces / 600g. (yes)

Cooking instructions:
Peel pears thinly (vitamins under the skin) and core. Juice in the juicer.

9.67 Plum Cake

Cancer preventive effect, dehydrates the body, stimulates digestion and binds fats in the intestine, good to fight loss of appetite, flatulence, inflammatory bowel disease, obesity, gout, stomach ulcers, stomach cramps, rheumatism, heartburn. Relieves pain, detoxifying, bactericide.
Cooking time approx. 1 hour
Calories p. portion: 502
6 portions
Allergens: AG

Quantity of ingredients
Curd cheese 20% 5/8 oz / 200g. (yes)
Wheat flour 7/8 lbs / 400g. (yes)
Plums 2,2 lbs / 1000g. (recommended)
Rapeseed oil 6 table spoons / 70g. (yes)
Honey 8 table spoons / 100g. (little)
Baking powder 1 package / 3g. (yes)
Salt 1 pinch / 1g. (little)
Cinnamon ground 1 teaspoon / 3g. (yes)
Cow's milk (whole milk 3.5% fat) 6 table spoons / 70g. (yes)

Cooking instructions:
Mix the flour, curd cheese, milk, oil, honey, salt and baking powder into a smooth dough. Keep the dough cool for 15 minutes to cool.
Lay out baking paper on a baking sheet and press the dough out to a bottom.
Now spread the plums evenly.
Sprinkle the cake with the cinnamon and bake for about 40 minutes at 190 ° C/374 °F.

9.68 Porcino mushroom-smoked tofu on toast bread

Good to fight loss of appetite, flatulence, improves digestion, improves thyroid function.
Do not eat together with spinach!
Cooking time approx. 1 hour
Calories p. portion: 169
2 portions
Allergens: AEMO

Quantity of ingredients
Olive oil 1/2 teaspoon / 5g. (yes)
Toast bread (whole grain) 6 slices / 30g. (yes)
Pepper (ground) 1 pinch / 0,5g. (yes)
Mustard Dijon 2 teaspoons / 6g. (yes)
Lemon peel 1 teaspoon / 2g. (yes)
Miso paste (soy bean paste) 1/4 cup / 50g. (yes)
Salt 1 pinch / 1g. (little)
Pickle 1 table spoon / 10g. (yes)
Soy Tofu smoked 5/8 oz / 200g. (yes)
Boletus mushroom 3/8 lbs - 6oz / 150g. (recommended)
Nutmeg 1 pinch / 1g. (yes)

Cooking instructions:
Use fresh or dried mushrooms. Soak the dried porcini mushrooms in 250 ml of hot water for 1 hour. Drain the mushrooms and cut small. Collect the soaking water and pour it through a fine sieve.
Heat olive oil lightly in a small, coated pan. Add the mushrooms, lightly salt, season with nutmeg and sauté briefly while stirring, add 6 tablespoons of soaking water, simmer gently until the liquid has evaporated.

Mix smoked tofu, the mushrooms, chopped pickle, soy cream, grated lemon peel and Dijon mustard with the cutter or the blender to a smooth spread.

Season the spread with salt and pepper. Serve on the toast bread slices.

9.69 Potato cream with herbs and fresh cheese

Good to fight loss of appetite, constipation, bloating and nausea. Improves digestion, supports urination, prevents cancer, forcing spleen, dissolves stagnation, relaxing and reassuring.
Cooking time approx. 25 min
Calories p. portion: 217
2 portions
Allergens: G

Quantity of ingredients
Black caraway 1 pinch / 0,5g. (yes)
Fresh cheese 3 oz / 80g. (yes)
Chives 1/2 bunch / 50g. (yes)
Pepper (ground) 1 pinch / 0,5g. (yes)
Salt 1 pinch / 1g. (little)
Dill 1/2 teaspoon / 2g. (yes)
Yogurt (natural, 1.5% fat) 2 table spoons / 45g. (yes)
Parsley 1 teaspoon / 4g. (yes)
Basil (fresh) 1 teaspoon / 4g. (yes)
Potato (mealy) 5/8 lbs - 8oz / 250g. (yes)

Cooking instructions:
Softly steam the potatoes in the pan, peel them and press through the potato press.
Mix cream cheese, yoghurt and herbs under the potatoes, season with salt, crushed black cumin and pepper.

9.70 Potato pancakes

Promotes spleen, reduces inflammation, improves digestion, regenerates skin, supports urination, calms nerves and stomach, laxative, antiparasitic.
Cooking time approx. 15 min
Calories p. portion: 893
1 portions
Allergens: ACG

Quantity of ingredients
Rapeseed oil 2 table spoons / 20g. (yes)
Potato (mealy) 5/8 lbs - 8oz / 250g. (yes)
Chicken egg 1 piece / 35g. (little)
Salt 1 pinch / 1g. (little)
Cream sour 20% 1/8 lbs - 2oz / 50g. (yes)
Salt 1 pinch / 1g. (little)
Herbs various 1 table spoon / 10g. (yes)
Wheat flour 1/2 oz / 10g. (yes)

Cooking instructions:
Grater the peeled potatoes finely, add the remaining ingredients, mix well and salt. Heat the oil and add small flat cakes to the pan with the spoon. Roast the potato pancakes on both sides crispy golden brown. Place them on the plate with sour cream, salt and sprinkle with herbs.

9.71 Potato with dandelion salad

Promotes spleen, reduces inflammation, improves digestion, regenerates skin, supports urinating, lowers cholesterol, detoxifying, reduces inflammation, forcing spleen and digestive system, detoxifying, dissolves
Cooking time approx. 25 min
Calories p. portion: 162
2 portions
Allergens: -

Quantity of ingredients
Sunflower oil 1 table spoon / 10g. (little)
Pepper white (ground) 1 pinch / 0,5g. (yes)
Potato 5/8 lbs - 8oz / 250g. (yes)
Dandelion (young plants) 1/4 lbs - 4oz / 125g. (yes)
Salt 1 pinch / 1g. (little)
Onion white 1/2 piece / 20g. (yes)

Cooking instructions:
Cook the potatoes in salted water and cut into thin slices. Finely chop the onion. Now season the potatoes with oil, salt and pepper and add the dandelion and mix.

9.72 Potato-basil soup

Reduces inflammation, improves digestion, supports urination, lowers cholesterol, reduces blood pressure, strengthens immune system, prevents cancer, reduces radiation damage, antioxidative, dissolves stagnation.
Cooking time approx. 25 min
Calories p. portion: 96
4 portions
Allergens: L

Quantity of ingredients
Olive oil 1 table spoon / 10g. (yes)
Celery root 1 piece / 500g. (yes)
Carrot 2 pieces / 100g. (yes)
Salt 1 pinch / 1g. (little)
Lemon 1 teaspoon / 3g. (yes)
Basil (fresh) 1 Bunch / 50g. (yes)
Ground 1 pinch / 1g. (yes)
Pepper (ground) 1 pinch / 0,5g. (yes)
Peppers powder 1 pinch / 1g. (yes)
Potato 4 pieces / 200g. (yes)
Water 2 cups / 450g. (yes)
Garlic 1 clove / 3g. (yes)
Sugar cane sugar 1 pinch / 1g. (little)

Cooking instructions:
Peeled and chopped 4 medium potatoes in a pot of hot water and 2 chopped medium carrots, a piece of celery root, a pinch of pepper, a pinch of ground cumin, crushed a small clove of garlic, a pinch of salt, 1 teaspoon of lemon juice, simmer until the Vegetables is soft.

Add 1 bunch finely chopped basil into one half of the soup and puree everything; stir in the other half of the basil; with rose paprika, a pinch of whole cane sugar, 1 tablespoon of olive oil or butter, freshly ground pepper, salt to taste.

9.73 Potato bags with wild herbs and tomato sauce

Promotes spleen, reduces inflammation, improves digestion, Good to fight loss of appetite, flatulence, inflammatory bowel disease, stimulates liver function, promotes urination, dissolves stagnation, detoxifies, supporting prostate disorders.
Cooking time approx. 45 min
Calories p. portion: 418
5 portions
Allergens: ACG

Quantity of ingredients
Wheat flour 5/8 oz / 200g. (yes)
Potato 1,4 lbs / 650g. (yes)
Black caraway 1 pinch / 1g. (yes)
Olive oil 1 table spoon / 10g. (yes)
Onion white 1 piece / 50g. (yes)
Garlic 1 piece / 2g. (yes)
Tomato puree 7/8 lbs / 400g. (yes)
Salt 1 pinch / 1g. (little)
Nutmeg 1 pinch / 0,2g. (yes)
Cream, sweet 30% 1 table spoon / 10g. (little)
Parsley 1/8 lbs - 2oz / 50g. (yes)
Pepper (ground) 1 pinch / 0,5g. (yes)
Salt 1 pinch / 1g. (little)
Nettles 1/8 lbs - 2oz / 50g. (yes)
Dandelion (young plants) 1 oz / 30g. (yes)
Yarrow 1 oz / 30g. (yes)
Chervil dried 1/2 oz / 10g. (yes)
Ribworttea 1/2 oz / 10g. (yes)
Pepper (ground) 1 pinch / 0,5g. (yes)
Olive oil 1 table spoon / 10g. (yes)
Emmental cheese 1/4 lbs / 100g. (little)
Pepper (ground) 1 pinch / 0,5g. (yes)
Salt (herbal) 1/2 teaspoon / 2g. (little)
Mayonnaise 50% 1 table spoon / 10g. (little)
Curd cheese 20% 4 table spoons / 40g. (yes)
Garlic 1 piece / 2g. (yes)
Chicken egg 1 piece / 60g. (little)

Cooking instructions:
Tomato sauce:
Heat oil. Roast diced onion briefly with crushed garlic. Add the tomato

puree and let it thicken for 2 minutes while stirring, season with salt and pepper and add the cream and place in a fireproof mold.

Potato Batter:
Cook the boiled potato, drain, peel and squeeze. Mix in a bowl with flour, Parmesan, egg and spices. Roll out the dough on a lightly floured work surface and cut into 5 cm squares.

Herb Stuffing:
Chop the herbs and mix with oil, garlic, curd cheese, mayonnaise, herb salt, crushed black cumin and pepper to a creamy mass.

Put on the pastry with a spoon in the middle. Fold into a triangle, press on the edge and let the pockets soak in plenty of salted water until they float up. Add to the tomatoes, sprinkle with the grated cheese and bake in the oven until golden brown.

9.74 Potatoes with wild garlic-curd cheese

Improves digestion, regenerates skin, supports urination, lowers cholesterol. Helps to fight stomach pressure, belching, diabetes, acute or chronic constipation of the intestine. Improves the flow characteristics of the blood.
Cooking time approx. 20 min
Calories p. portion: 254
2 portions
Allergens: G

Quantity of ingredients
Wild garlic (garlic spinach) 2 handful / 30g. (yes)
Salt 1 pinch / 1g. (little)
Salt 1 pinch / 0,1g. (little)
Potato 3/4 lbs / 300g. (yes)
Curd cheese 20% 5/8 lbs - 8oz / 250g. (yes)
Yogurt (natural, 1.5% fat) 2 table spoons / 20g. (yes)

Cooking instructions:
Cook potatoes in salted water and peel.
Wash he wild garlic leaves and carefully dried and cut into fine strips. Mix the cottage cheese, yogurt and salt and mix in the chopped wild garlic pieces. Serve with the potatoes.
In the season in which no wild garlic grows the wild garlic pesto can be used.

9.75 Pumpkin curry

Promotes digestion and sweating, Dissolves stagnation, strengthens lungs and spleen, diuretic, reduces blood glucose, forcing spleen and digestive system, detoxifying, strengthens the muscles and bones.
Cooking time approx. 20 min
Calories p. portion: 193
3 portions
Allergens: -

Quantity of ingredients
Cardamom 1 pinch / 1g. (yes)
Pumpkin 3/4 lbs / 300g. (yes)
Curry 1 pinch / 1g. (yes)
Salt 1 pinch / 1g. (little)
Parsley 1 table spoon / 7g. (yes)
Olive oil 2 table spoons / 30g. (yes)
Turmeric (yellow root) 1 pinch / 1g. (yes)
Pepper (ground) 1 pinch / 0,5g. (yes)
Rice (whole grain) 1/2 cup / 60g. (recommended)
Water 3 cups / 300g. (yes)
Salt 1 pinch / 1g. (little)
Water 1/4 cup / 50g. (yes)
Coriander 1 pinch / 1g. (yes)

Cooking instructions:
Heat olive oil in pan. Steam the pumpkin cut in cubes, season with cilantro, pepper and curry, simmer with a little water, salt with sea salt, add chopped parsley with cardamom and turmeric, simmer on a small fire for about 10 minutes, depending on the pumpkin, the pumpkin should still be firm.
Place the rice in salted water, bring to the boil and let it simmer over low heat for about 15 minutes.

9.76 Pumpkin soup

Promotes digestion, forcing spleen and stomach, reduces blood pressure, strengthens immune system, prevents cancer, reduces radiation damage, improves digestion, regenerates skin, lowers cholesterol, reduces blood glucose, protects liver.
Cooking time approx. 1 hour
Calories p. portion: 105
3 portions
Allergens: -

Quantity of ingredients
Olive oil 1 table spoon / 10g. (yes)
Salt 1 pinch / 1g. (little)
Potato 2 pieces / 120g. (yes)
Anise (Common Fennel) 1 pinch / 1g. (yes)
Parsley 1 table spoon / 7g. (yes)
Water 1 cup / 120g. (yes)
Onion white 1 piece / 50g. (yes)
Carrot 2 pieces / 100g. (yes)
Pumpkin 3/4 lbs / 300g. (yes)

Cooking instructions:
Add the olive oil to the pan, add the diced pumpkin, diced carrots and potatoes. Roast them shortly, add the finely chopped onion, fill with water, add enough water to cover the vegetables at least 3 finger-widths. Boil at low heat.
Season with sea salt, add small cutted parsley, a pinch of anise (little). Allow to simmer for about 35 minutes. Then purée the soup and add some water, depending on the consistency of the soup.

9.77 Quick zucchini soup

Diuretic, supports urination. Strengthens gastrointestinal function, expands blood vessels, prevents cancer, prevents diseases (in the elderly). Stimulates liver function, detoxifying.
Cooking time approx. 10 min
Calories p. portion: 42
4 portions
Allergens: -

Quantity of ingredients
Chives 1 teaspoon / 3g. (yes)
Water 2 cup / 400g. (yes)
Parsley 1 table spoon / 7g. (yes)
Corn germ oil 2 table spoons / 6g. (little)
Onion white 1 piece / 50g. (yes)
Zucchini 2-3 pieces / 500g. (recommended)

Cooking instructions:
Fry chopped onion in oil. Add sliced zucchini and sauté well. Pour with water. Chop parsley and chives, add and puree everything.

9.78 Radish with sugar

Promotes digestion, detoxifying, improves blood circulation, supports urination, reduces thirst, strengthens body cells, dissolves stagnation, relieves weakness, promotes spleen, calms stomach,
Cooking time approx. 5 min
Calories p. portion: 46
2 portions
Allergens: -

Quantity of ingredients
Radish (white, green, purple-red) 1 piece / 400g. (yes)
Sugar brown 1 teaspoon / 4g. (little)

Cooking instructions:
Grate the radish and sprinkle with sugar.

9.79 Raw celery salad

Refreshing, forcing spleen, provides Vitamin C, strengthens digestive system, detoxifying, improves blood circulation, strengthens liver and kidney, detoxifying, strengthens the muscles, promotes weight loss.
Cooking time approx. 15 min
Calories p. portion: 590
1 portions
Allergens: HLN

Quantity of ingredients
Celery root 1/4 piece / 125g. (yes)
Celery sticks 2 branches / 30g. (yes)
Salt 1 pinch / 1g. (little)
Pepper (ground) 1 pinch / 0,5g. (yes)
Lemon 1/2 cup / 50g. (yes)
Orange juice 1/2 cup / 60g. (little)
Peppers powder 1 pinch / 1g. (yes)
Sesame oil 4 table spoons / 40g. (little)
Almond puree 2 table spoons / 20g. (little)

Cooking instructions:
Finely grate the celeriac; cut the celeriac into small pieces; celery leaves, cut into small pieces, blanch and combine everything.
Dressing: sesame oil, almond paste, pepper, salt, lemon and fresh orange juice, stir well some rose paprika; mix with the celery and let it pass through.

9.80 Refreshing cucumber soup with potatoes

Diuretic, detoxifying, suppresses conversion of sugar into fat, lowers cholesterol, prevents cancer, reduces inflammation, improves digestion, lowers cholesterol, dissolves stagnation, improves blood circulation, stimulates appetite.
Cooking time approx. 15 min
Calories p. portion: 148
3 portions
Allergens: GN

Quantity of ingredients
Salt 1 pinch / 1g. (little)
Lemon 1/2 piece / 25g. (yes)
Onion (spring onion) 3 pieces / 60g. (yes)
Sesame oil 1 table spoon / 10g. (little)
Nutmeg 1 pinch / 1g. (yes)
Cucumber 2 pieces / 500g. (yes)
Dill 1 table spoon / 15g. (yes)
Cream, sweet 30% 1 table spoon / 10g. (little)
Potato 4 pieces / 300g. (yes)
Pepper (ground) 1 pinch / 0,5g. (yes)

Cooking instructions:
Sauté sesame oil, chopped potatoes, plenty of spring onions in a hot pot; add pepper, a little nutmeg, salt, lemon juice, hot water, diced cucumber; simmer for about 10 minutes and then puree; add some sweet cream as you like, fresh dill.

Variation: Add a little chili, oregano, thyme or rosemary to soften the cooling effect.

9.81 Rhubarb cake with sprinkles

Laxative, antipyretic. Protects the digestive system. Detoxifying, affects anorexia, good to fight flatulence, inflammatory bowel disease, brittle nails and hair. Relieves pain, detoxifying, against dry skin, acne, eczema.

Cooking time approx. 1 1/2 hours
Calories p. portion: 476
8 portions
Allergens: AG

Quantity of ingredients
Cinnamon ground 2 pinches / 1g. (yes)
Salt 1 pinch / 1g. (little)
Lemon peel 1 piece / 3g. (yes)
Cow's milk (whole milk 3.5% fat) 1 cup / 200g. (yes)
Honey 5 table spoons / 50g. (little)
Honey 2 teaspoons / 5g. (little)
Vanilla sugar natural 2 pinches / 1g. (little)
Yeast 1 oz / 30g. (little)
Wheat flour 3/4 lbs / 300g. (yes)
Margarine 1/4 lbs - 4oz / 120g. (little)
Sunflower oil 2 teaspoons / 5g. (little)
Rhubarb 2,2 lbs / 800g. (yes)
Wheat flour 7/8 lbs / 400g. (yes)

Cooking instructions:
Mix flour, grated lemon peel and salt.
Heat milk gently and mix with yeast and honey.
Then add the flour mixture and the oil and knead vigorously. Cover the dough and let it rise in a warm place until it reaches twice the amount. (about 30 minutes)
For the sprinkles, mix flour with vanilla and cinnamon, then add honey and margarine and crumble to a crumbly mass. Keep the sprinkles dough cool.
Lay out a baking sheet with parchment paper.
Knead the dough for the bottom again, roll it out, place it on the baking sheet and let it rise for another 10 minutes.
Clean the rhubarb, wash it, halve lengthwise and cut into pieces of approx. 3 cm. Spread the pieces on the rolled out dough and crumble the sprinkles over the cake.
Place the cake in the preheated oven at 175 ° C and bake for about 40 minutes.

9.82 Ribbon noodles with leaf spinach

Promotes digestion, improves blood circulation, forcing spleen and intestine, improves pancreatic function, good to fight loss of appetite, flatulence, inflammatory bowel disease, obesity, stomach ulcers, stomach cramps, rheumatism, heartburn, twelffinger intestinal ulcers.
Cooking time approx. 45 min
Calories p. portion: 722
2 portions
Allergens: ACG

Quantity of ingredients
Thyme dried 1/2 teaspoon / 2g. (yes)
Basil (fresh) 1/2 teaspoon / 2g. (yes)
Crème fraiche cheese 1/2 teaspoon / 6g. (little)
Black caraway 1 pinch / 1g. (yes)
Oregano dried 1/2 teaspoon / 2g. (yes)
Cream, sweet 30% 1/2 cup / 100g. (little)
Nutmeg 1 pinch / 0,5g. (yes)
Parmesan 1/2 oz / 20g. (yes)
Pine nuts 1 table spoon / 15g. (yes)
Pepper (ground) 1 pinch / 0,5g. (yes)
Noodles (wheat, ribbon noodles) with egg 5/8 oz / 200g. (little)
Onion (spring onion) 1 piece / 20g. (yes)
Salt 1 pinch / 1g. (little)
Spinach 5/8 lbs - 8oz / 250g. (yes)
Olive oil 1 table spoon / 15g. (yes)

Cooking instructions:
Put the dripping wet spinach together with a little salt for 3 minutes ina pot, then drain in a sieve. Then finely cut.
Boil tagliatelle in plenty of salted water.
Heat the oil in a skillet and fry the spring onions rings. Add cream, crème fraiche, thyme, basil, oregano and nutmeg. Stir in the sauce while stirring. Add the spinach, heat briefly, season with nutmeg, salt and pepper.
Drain pasta and mix with the spinach. Season with salt and pepper.
Portion noodles and serve with parmesan and pine nuts. Sprinkle the black cumin over it.

9.83 Rice with parsnips

Rich in vitamins, minerals potassium and zinc. Good to fight blood circulation disorders, thrombose, risk of embolism, high blood pressure, a headache, heart attack and stroke, yeast infections.
Cooking time approx. 45 min
Calories p. portion: 206
3 portions
Allergens: -

Quantity of ingredients
Olive oil 1 table spoon / 10g. (yes)
Salt 1 pinch / 1g. (little)
Water 1 1/2 cups / 200g. (yes)

Rice variety any 1 cup / 120g. (little)
Sage 1 teaspoon / 3g. (yes)
Parsnip 3-4 pieces / 450g. (yes)

Cooking instructions:
Peel the parsnips and cut into slices. Fry for a short time in oil. Add the rice and fry again for a short time. Add the water and cook it at least 30 min. Sprinkle with fresh chopped sage.

9.84 Rice with stewed vegetables

Reduces blood pressure, strengthens immune system, extremely low fat content, good to fight blood circulation disorders, thrombose, risk of embolism, a headache, heart attack and stroke. Is diuretic.
Cooking time approx. 20 min
Calories p. portion: 166
2 portions
Allergens: L

Quantity of ingredients
Water 1/2 cup / 0g. (yes)
Cress 2 table spoons / 20g. (yes)
Rice variety any 1/2 cup / 60g. (little)
Celery sticks 1/2 piece / 5g. (yes)
Linseed oil 1 dash / 3g. (yes)
Lemon peel 1 piece / 3g. (yes)
Champignon 1/2 cup / 50g. (yes)
Water 3 cups / 300g. (yes)
Carrot 2 pieces / 180g. (yes)

Cooking instructions:
Cook rice according to basic recipe with a piece of lemon peel. Steam chopped carrots, celery and mushrooms until soft.
Then sprinkle with cress. Then add a dash of high quality cold oil.

9.85 Roasted barley patties

Improves digestion, lowers cholesterol, good to fight diarrhea, ulceration, joint pain. Promotes spleen and liver, reduces blood pressure, strengthens immune system, stimulates liver function.
Cooking time approx. 1 1/2 hours
Calories p. portion: 398
3 portions
Allergens: ACN

Quantity of ingredients
Carrot 1 piece / 120g. (yes)
Peppers powder 1 pinch / 1g. (yes)
Potato 1 piece / 140g. (yes)
Barley grouts 1 cup / 120g. (yes)
Lemon 1/2 piece / 15g. (yes)
Champignon 2-3 pieces / 25g. (yes)
Chicken egg 1 piece / 55g. (little)
Onion white 1 piece / 50g. (yes)
Parsley 2 table spoons / 15g. (yes)
Sesame oil 2 table spoons / 50g. (little)
Bread roll 1 piece / 35g. (little)
Ginger fresh 1/2 teaspoon / 1g. (yes)
Pepper (ground) 1 pinch / 0,5g. (yes)
Water 1 1/2 cups / 250g. (yes)
Salt 1 pinch / 1g. (little)

Cooking instructions:
Preparation:
Place 2 large cups of hot water in a saucepan; add 1 large cup of barley porridge; simmer for 2 minutes while stirring; then let it swell for 20 minutes on the switched off stove; take down and let cool.
Cook in boiling water 1 large potato, chopped and cut.
Soak 1 roll in hot water and squeeze well.
Then: Mix the barley groats and crushed the potato. Add 1 grated carrot, 2 - 3 chopped mushrooms, 1 egg, 1 finely chopped onion, 1/2 teaspoon grated ginger, a pinch of pepper, a pinch of salt, a little lemon juice, chopped parsley, plenty of rose paprika; knead well and form patties; heat sesame oil in a hot pan; fry the patties for about 15 minutes over a gentle heat; turn at half time.
Also fits well: lettuce, soybean vegetables.

9.86 Rosemary Potatoes

Reduces Inflammation, improves digestion, regenerates skin, supports urination, lowers cholesterol. Rosemary stimulates digestion, strengthens lung, promotes spleen and kidney, dries out.
Cooking time approx. 30 min
Calories p. portion: 188
2 portions
Allergens: -

Quantity of ingredients
Potato 6-8 pieces / 420g. (yes)
Salt (herbal) 1 pinch / 1g. (little)
Olive oil 1 table spoon / 10g. (yes)
Rosemary 1 teaspoon / 2g. (yes)

Cooking instructions:
Cut the potatoes into halfs, apply a little olive oil on the cut surface, then salt, sprinkle 2 - 3 rosemary needles on the potatoes.
Place the potatoes on the baking tray and bake them in the preheated oven for approx. 25 minutes to 190°C/374°F.

9.87 Russian kasha with white cabbage

Promotes digestion, relieves pain, detoxifying, promotes digestion, stimulates appetite, dissolves stagnation, stimulates blood production and metabolism, reduces fat.
Cooking time approx. 30 min
Calories p. portion: 250
2 portions
Allergens: AG

Quantity of ingredients
Nutmeg 1 pinch / 1g. (yes)
Ground 1 pinch / 2g. (yes)
Butter Bio 1 teaspoon / 3g. (little)
White cabbage Handful / 20g. (recommended)
Water 1 1/2 cups / 240g. (yes)
Buckwheat whole grain 1 cup / 130g. (recommended)
Salt 1 pinch / 1g. (little)
Parsley 1 table spoon / 10g. (yes)

Cooking instructions:
Roast buckwheat golden yellow; add boiling water, heat till it boils briefly and then let it swell until soft; Grate the white cabbage finely and fold in. Season with nutmeg, a little salt; some parsley, cumin and butter at the end.

9.88 Salmon on tomato-spinach

Promotes bowel movement, improves blood circulation, forcing spleen and bowel, strengthens blood, reduces inflammation, improves digestion, regenerates skin, supports urination, lowers cholesterol, promotes sweating, dissolves stagnation.

Cooking time approx. 1 hour
Calories p. portion: 365
6 portions
Allergens: D

Quantity of ingredients
Pine nuts 4 table spoons / 40g. (yes)
Leek 1/4 lbs - 4oz / 120g. (yes)
Salt 1 pinch / 1g. (little)
Pepper white (ground) 1 pinch / 0,5g. (yes)
Potato 1,1 lbs / 500g. (yes)
Salt 1 pinch / 1g. (little)
Salmon 1,3 lbs / 600g. (yes)
Rapeseed oil 2 teaspoons / 24g. (yes)
Tomato 1/4 lbs - 4oz / 100g. (yes)
Salt 1 pinch / 1g. (little)
Olive oil 4 table spoons / 40g. (yes)
Spinach 1,5 lbs / 700g. (yes)

Cooking instructions:
Peel the potato and cut into cubes, cook in salted water.
Cut the salmon into portions and fry slowly and evenly in a frying pan from both sides, seasoned with salt and pepper, then add the pine nuts and lightly roast.
Blanch spinach in salted water.
Lightly sweat the finely chopped leek with a little rapeseed oil, add the blanched spinach and heat evenly.
Just before serving, add the halved cocktail tomatoes to the spinach and season the vegetables well with salt and pepper.
Arrange the spinach and leek tomato bed with the potatoes, add the salmon and sprinkle with the salted pine nuts.
Drizzle with a little olive oil and serve the dish.

9.89 Scrambled eggs with leaf salad olives and tomatoes

Calms nerves and stomach, relieves fatigue, regulates gastrointestinal function, promotes digestion, stimulates liver function, detoxifying, helps to digest fat, supports urination, reduces blood pressure.
Cooking time approx. 10 min
Calories p. portion: 419
1 portions
Allergens: C

Quantity of ingredients
Pepper (ground) 1 pinch / 0,5g. (yes)
Lettuce 2 leaves / 5g. (yes)
Turmeric (yellow root) 1 pinch / 1g. (yes)
Olive oil 1 table spoon / 10g. (yes)
Basil (fresh) 2-3 leaves / 2g. (yes)
Olives 6 pieces / 10g. (yes)
Salt 1 pinch / 1g. (little)
Chicken egg 2-3 pieces / 180g. (little)
Parsley 1/2 teaspoon / 5g. (yes)
Tomato 1 piece / 50g. (yes)

Cooking instructions:
Heat olive oil in the pan. Cut the tomato into a slice. Pluck salad into small pieces. Briefly fry tomatoes, lettuce and olives. Meanwhile mix eggs with salt and spices with a fork.
Pour the egg and spices into the pan. Stir with a wooden spoon until it reaches the desired consistency.
Spices and herbs: turmeric, parsley, basil, black cumin
Variation: zucchini, rocket

9.90 Scrambled eggs with rocket and herbs

Calms nerves and stomach, promotes digestion, detoxifying, strengthens bodily fluids production, promotes perspiration, reduces blood lipids, stimulates, dissolves stagnation, stimulates liver function, harmonizes liver and spleen, strengthens eyesight, detoxifying.
Cooking time approx. 10 min
Calories p. portion: 360
1 portions
Allergens: CG

Quantity of ingredients
Chicken egg 2 pieces / 120g. (little)
Savory 1 pinch / 0,5g. (yes)
Butter Bio 2 table spoons / 20g. (little)
Ginger fresh 1 knife tip / 1g. (yes)
Oregano dried 1 teaspoon / 2g. (yes)
Rucola 2 handful / 30g. (yes)
Parsley 2 table spoons / 16g. (yes)
Pepper (ground) 1 pinch / 0,5g. (yes)
Coriander 1 pinch / 1g. (yes)

Cooking instructions:
Melt a piece of butter in a hot pan; add fine cutted ginger and roast it shortly. Mix in 1 egg whipped, pepper freshly ground, a pinch of coriander, bean cabbage, some salt, parsley chopped, rocket and oregano cut into small pieces until the egg stalls, but still juicy. Garnish: millet, polenta, potatoes, toasted bread. The dish is wholesome, without carbohydrate.

9.91 Sliced chicken with walnuts and sherry

Strengthens blood, strengthens bone marrow, strengthens gastrointestinal function, expands blood vessels, prevents cancer, promotes perspiration, reduces blood lipids, stimulates.
Cooking time approx. 25 min
Calories p. portion: 304
4 portions
Allergens: EGHN

Quantity of ingredients
Walnuts 2 table spoons / 25g. (yes)
Ginger fresh 1/2 teaspoon / 2g. (yes)
Salt 1 pinch / 1g. (little)
Water 6 cups / 550g. (yes)
Rice (whole grain) 1 cup / 120g. (recommended)
Black fungus mushroom 4 pieces / 3g. (yes)
Shiitake, dried 4 pieces / 5g. (yes)
Peppers powder 1 pinch / 1g. (yes)
Chicken meat 3/4 lbs / 300g. (little)
Sesame, white 1 teaspoon / 2g. (recommended)
Onion (shallot) 2 pieces / 40g. (yes)
Butter Bio 2 table spoons / 35g. (little)
Soy sauce 1 dash / 3g. (yes)
Salt 1 pinch / 1g. (little)

Cooking instructions:
Heat butter or sesame oil in a hot pan; Sauté walnuts, copious grated ginger, chopped shallots or onions; Add the salt and the sliced chicken and sauté everything; Rose paprika, roasted sesame, soaked black fungus, shiitake mushrooms or mushrooms; with a shot sherry; infuse with water; Simmer for 5 to 10 minutes until the meat is cooked; Season with soy sauce.
Place the rice in salted water, heat till it boils and let it simmer over low heat for about 15 minutes.

9.92 Spicy avocado cream with cottage cheese

Anti-inflammatory, good to fight swelling, pain and itching, forcing spleen and digestive system, detoxifying, bactericide.
Cooking time approx. 15 min
Calories p. portion: 614
4 portions
Allergens: G

Quantity of ingredients
Pepper (ground) 1 pinch / 0,5g. (yes)
Bread with carob kernel flour 8 slices / 200g. (yes)
Salt 1 pinch / 1g. (little)
Peppers powder 1 pinch / 1g. (yes)
Cottage cheese 1 cup / 250g. (yes)
Avocado 2 pieces / 600g. (yes)
Olive oil 1 table spoon / 10g. (yes)
Lemon juice 1/2 piece / 15g. (yes)
Herbs various 1 table spoon / 7g. (yes)

Cooking instructions:
Peel, core and purée avocados; add plenty of ground pepper, salt, lemon juice, rose paprika, a few drops of oil, chili, fresh chopped herbs, a pinch of salt; cottage cheese (about the same amount as avocado cream), carefully submerge.
Goes well with: Potatoes and millet, with which the avocado cream in combination with vegetable dishes, legumes or lettuce leaves a delicious meal. It is also very good as an appetizer, as a souvenir at parties and as a morning meal in the summer together with a mild dish of lentils or Adzuki beans and grated radish.

9.93 Spicy Tofu Vegetable Pan

Forcing spleen, relieves constipation, detoxifying, reduces inflammation, improves blood circulation, promotes sweating, dissolves stagnation, reduces flatulence, reduces blood pressure, strengthens immune system, prevents cancer, reduces radiation damage.
Cooking time approx. 25 min
Calories p. portion: 241
4 portions
Allergens: EN

Quantity of ingredients
Fennel 1 piece / 250g. (yes)

Leek 1 piece / 200g. (yes)
Turmeric (yellow root) 1 pinch / 1g. (yes)
Water 6 cups / 500g. (yes)
Salt 1 pinch / 1g. (little)
Pepper (ground) 1 pinch / 0,5g. (yes)
Soy sauce 1 dash / 3g. (yes)
Sesame oil 2 table spoons / 20g. (little)
Salt 1 pinch / 1g. (little)
Soy Tofu 1 package / 120g. (yes)
Lemon juice 1 dach / 1g. (yes)
Rice (whole grain) 1 cup / 120g. (recommended)
Carrot 2 pieces / 100g. (yes)

Cooking instructions:
Heat sesame oil in a hot wok or a hot pan; fry the chopped carrots, fennel and leek slices; salt, a dash of lemon juice, turmeric, tofu cubes roast for 1 - 2 minutes.
Add the pepper and cook covered for about 5 minutes; drizzle with soy sauce.
Place the rice in salted water, heat till it boils and let it simmer over low heat for about 15 minutes.

9.94 Spinach with Tahini

Promotes bowel movement, improves blood circulation, forcing spleen and bowel, improves pancreatic function. Improves digestion, regenerates skin, supports urination, lowers cholesterol. Gentle laxative.
Cooking time approx. 20 min
Calories p. portion: 150
4 portions
Allergens: N

Quantity of ingredients
Potato 1,1 lbs / 500g. (yes)
Water 1 cup / 25g. (yes)
Spinach 2,2 lbs / 800g. (yes)
Sesame paste (Tahini) 2 table spoons / 20g. (yes)
Salt 1 pinch / 0,2g. (little)

Cooking instructions:
Cook potatoes and peel. Heat water. Blanch spinach. Shake off water and let it dry and stir with sesame.

9.95 Strawberry soup with melons

Relieves pain and inflammation in rheumatism. Diuretic, helps to fight constipation.
Cooking time approx. 5 min
Calories p. portion: 87
2 portions
Allergens: -

Quantity of ingredients
Cantaloupe 5/8 oz / 200g. (yes)
Lemon peel 1/4 teaspoon / 1g. (yes)
Strawberry Juice 1/3 cup / 70g. (yes)
Strawberries 3/4 lbs / 300g. (yes)

Cooking instructions:
Puree strawberries (fresh or frozen) and strawberry juice with the blender, mix in a little sugar.
Cut melon pulp into small pieces.
Arrange strawberry soup in portions. Put the melon cubes in the sweet soup.

9.96 Strawberry yoghurt and almond puree mix

Relieves pain and inflammation in rheumatism. Good to fight acute or chronic constipation of the intestine. Little laxative. Relieves pain, detoxifying, bactericide.
Cooking time approx. 5 min
Calories p. portion: 134
3 portions
Allergens: GH

Quantity of ingredients
Acerola fruit nectar or powder 1 teaspoon / 2g. (little)
Almond puree 2 teaspoons / 6g. (little)
Honey 1 teaspoon / 3g. (little)
Strawberries 1,5 lbs / 700g. (yes)
Yogurt (natural, 1.5% fat) 5/8 oz / 200g. (yes)

Cooking instructions:
Puree yoghurt, strawberries, acerola, honey and almond paste in a blender.

9.97 Tea from anise

Anise (wild fennel) promotes digestion, forcing spleen and stomach.
Cooking time approx. 15 min
Calories p. portion: 3
4 portions
Allergens: -

Quantity of ingredients
Anise (Common Fennel) 1 teaspoon / 3g. (yes)
Water 2 cup / 500g. (yes)

Cooking instructions:
Heat the water till it boils and put it aside. Add anise.
10 min. to let go.
Pour through a tea strainer. Sweet to taste with honey.
In order to achieve a salutary effect, you should drink 2 cups of anise tea per day.

9.98 Tea from coriander

Coriander promotes digestion, diaphoretic.
Cooking time approx. 10 min
Calories p. portion: 2
4 portions
Allergens: -

Quantity of ingredients
Water 2 cup / 500g. (yes)
Coriander 1 teaspoon / 3g. (yes)

Cooking instructions:
Heat the water till it boils and put it aside. Add coriander and 10 min. to let go. Sweet to taste with honey. Strain when pouring.

9.99 Tea from elderberry blossom tea

Good, if you have a sore throat. Good to fight colds. Promotes urination, good to fight flu, urinary stones, concentration weakness, blackheads, hay fever, rheumatism. Strengthen the immune system, diaphoretic.
Cooking time approx. 10 min
Calories p. portion: 7
4 portions
Allergens: -

Quantity of ingredients
Water 2 cup / 500g. (yes)
Elderberry blossom tee 4 teaspoons / 12g. (yes)

Cooking instructions:
Heat the water till it boils and put it aside. Add holligan flowers and 10 min. to let go. Sweet to taste with honey.
Strain when pouring.

9.100   Tea from fenugreek (Trigonella foenum-graecum)

Good to fight Bloating, helps to figt nervous digestive problems, promotes the expectoration of mucus, regulates the blood glucose level.
Cooking time approx. 10 min
Calories p. portion: 0
4 portions
Allergens: -

Quantity of ingredients
Fenugreek (Trigonella foenum-graecum) 2-4 teaspoons / 9g. (yes)
Water 2 cup / 500g. (yes)

Cooking instructions:
Brew the fenugreek with boiling water and let it cover for about 10 minutes. Strain the tea and drink warm.

9.101   Tea from ginger with honey

Honey relieves pain, detoxifying, bactericide.
Fresh ginger encourages digestion, detoxifying, strengthens bodily production, promotes perspiration, reduces blood lipids, stimulates, dissolves stagnation.
Cooking time approx. 30 min
Calories p. portion: 5
4 portions
Allergens: -

Quantity of ingredients
Water 2 cup / 500g. (yes)
Ginger fresh 1 teaspoon / 3g. (yes)
Honey 2 teaspoons / 6g. (little)

Cooking instructions:
Heat the water till it boils and put it aside. Add ginger and 20-30 min. to let go. Sweet to taste with honey.

9.102 Tea from ground

Cumin promotes digestion, reduces flatulence.
Cooking time approx. 10 min
Calories p. portion: 2
4 portions
Allergens: -

Quantity of ingredients
Ground 1 teaspoon / 3g. (yes)
Water 2 cup / 500g. (yes)

Cooking instructions:
Heat the water till it boils and put it aside. Add crushed cumin and leave for 10 min. to let go. Sweet to taste with honey. Strain when pouring. Drink 1 cup 2 times a day.

9.103 Tea from Marjoram

Promotes the digestion of fatty foods. Diuretic effect. Antibacterial effect in the climacteric period. Good to fight menopausal complaints.
Cooking time approx. 10 min
Calories p. portion: 0
4 portions
Allergens: -

Quantity of ingredients
Water 2 cup / 500g. (yes)
Marjoram 2 teaspoons / 6g. (yes)

Cooking instructions:
Heat the water till it boils and put it aside. Add marjoram and 10 min. to let go. Sweet to taste with honey. Strain when pouring.

9.104 Tea mixture against intestinal inertia

Promote digestion, Strengthens the stomach, Diuretic and generally powerful, good to fight loss of appetite, improves digestion and stomach ailments.
Cooking time approx. 20 min

Calories p. portion: 1
8 portions
Allergens: -

Quantity of ingredients
Gentian root 1 table spoon / 20g. (yes)
Water 4 cup / 1000g. (yes)
Blackthorn (Sloe) 1 table spoon / 20g. (yes)
Kalmus 1 table spoon / 20g. (yes)

Cooking instructions:
Preparation:
Mix gentian 20 g kalmus 20 g and blackthorn 20 g.
Preparation: 1 tablespoon of the mixture to 1 cup as an infusion, let stand for 15-20 minutes.
Use: Drink 1 cup warm in the morning and evening.

9.105 Thick pea soup

Supports urination, detoxifying, dissolves stagnation, improves blood circulation, strengthens liver and kidney, strengthens immune system.
Cooking time approx. 2-3 hours
Calories p. portion: 123
3 portions
Allergens: AN

Quantity of ingredients
Sesame oil 1 table spoon / 20g. (little)
Water 2 1/4 cups / 550g. (yes)
Peas, green 3/8 lbs - 6oz / 150g. (yes)
Ginger fresh 1/2 teaspoon / 1g. (yes)
Onion white 1/2 piece / 25g. (yes)
Salt 1 pinch / 1g. (little)
Oat meal 1 table spoon / 15g. (recommended)
Ground 1/2 teaspoon / 1g. (yes)
Parsley 1 stem / 2g. (yes)

Cooking instructions:
Soak dried peas before cooking. Sauté sesame oil, onion, a little oatmeal, ginger and cumin in a hot pot; add the peas and simmer for 2-3 hours; add salt at the end and puree with a blender; garnish with parsley.

9.106 Tomato soup

Promotes digestion, helps to digest fat, supports urination, reduces blood pressure, dissolves stagnation. Contains unsaturated fatty acids, is antioxidativ.
Cooking time approx. 10 min
Calories p. portion: 100
2 portions
Allergens: -

Quantity of ingredients
Cinnamon ground 1 pinch / 1g. (yes)
Salt 1 pinch / 1g. (little)
Onion white 1 piece / 60g. (yes)
Pepper (ground) 1 pinch / 0,5g. (yes)
Peppers powder 1 pinch / 1g. (yes)
Olive oil 1 table spoon / 15g. (yes)
Water 5/8 lbs - 8oz / 250g. (yes)
Tomato 6 pieces / 250g. (yes)
Basil (fresh) 1 teaspoon / 2g. (yes)

Cooking instructions:
Roast the onion in a pot. Salt and spices. Briefly roast. Put washed and quartered tomatoes in the pan. Stir and sauté briefly. Add a quart of water and heat till it boils. Cook for a quarter of an hour and puree.

9.107 Turkey breast with vegetables (Asian)

Strengthens blood, strengthens bone marrow, dissolves stagnation, promotes digestion and is goo to fight high blood pressure. Rice to drain the body at overweight and high blood pressure.
Cooking time approx. 45 min
Calories p. portion: 535
2 portions
Allergens: AEN

Quantity of ingredients
Peppers 1/2 piece / 10g. (yes)
Water 6 cups / 240g. (yes)
Turkey breast meat 5/8 oz / 200g. (little)
Ginger fresh 1/3 inch / 3g. (yes)
Garlic 1 piece / 2g. (yes)
Rice variety any 1 cup / 120g. (little)
Turmeric (yellow root) 1 pinch / 2g. (yes)

Onion (spring onion) 2 pieces / 40g. (yes)
Champignon 8 pieces / 30g. (yes)
Sesame oil 2 table spoons / 20g. (little)
Soy sauce 1 table spoon / 12g. (yes)
Curry 1 pinch / 2g. (yes)
Soy sauce 2 table spoons / 20g. (yes)
Cashews 2 teaspoons / 25g. (yes)
Wheat flour 2 teaspoons / 15g. (yes)

Cooking instructions:
Cook the rice in salted water.
Cut the turkey meat into thin strips. Peel and dice the ginger and garlic. Put together with the meat strips in a bowl.
Mix 1 tbsp of soy sauce with the wheat starch and stir until smooth. Add to the meat and marinate for 30 minutes.
Wash spring onions and peppers, clean and cut into small pieces.
Clean and quarter the mushrooms.
Put one tablespoon of sesame oil in a pan and sauté and warm the marinated turkey. Now add the remaining oil to the pan and fry the other vegetables in it. Now add the meat and season with soy sauce and spices. Serve with the rice. Sprinkle the cashews over the dish before serving.

9.108   Vanilla cream with berries

Weakness, chronic constipation of the intestine, weight loss.
Strengthens the defense. Good to fight fungi infections.
Cooking time approx. 15 min
Calories p. portion: 278
4 portions
Allergens: G

Quantity of ingredients
Acerola fruit nectar or powder 1 teaspoon / 2g. (little)
Cream (30% fat) 1/4 lbs - 4oz / 125g. (little)
Curd cheese 20% 7/8 lbs / 400g. (yes)
Yogurt (natural, 1.5% fat) 3/8 lbs - 6oz / 150g. (yes)
Sugar brown 2 teaspoons / 8g. (little)
Strawberries 1/4 lbs - 4oz / 100g. (yes)
Blackberry´s 1/4 lbs - 4oz / 100g. (yes)
Blueberry 1/4 lbs - 4oz / 100g. (yes)
Vanilla sugar natural 3 package / 3g. (little)
Raspberry 1/4 lbs - 4oz / 100g. (yes)

Cooking instructions:
Mix the curd cheese, yoghurt, sugar, acerola and vanilla sugar with a hand mixer or whisk until smooth. Beat the whipped cream very stiff, mix it under the cream. Arrange vanilla cream in portions with the berries.

9.109 Vanilla pudding

Helps to fight constipation.
Cooking time approx. 10 min
Calories p. portion: 254
2 portions
Allergens: G

Quantity of ingredients
Sugar white 1 table spoon / 12g. (little)
Pudding powder vanilla 1 package / 37g. (yes)
Cow's milk (whole milk 3.5% fat) 2 cups / 500g. (yes)

Cooking instructions:
Give 3-5 tablespoons of milk into a cup, bring the rest in a pot to boil. Pour the powdered pudding into the cup and stir until free of lumpy. As soon as the milk boils, add the mixture and simmer under low heat for about 3 minutes.
Divide into prepared bowls.

9.110 Vegetable bowl with Provencal pistou

Promotes spleen and liver, reduces blood pressure, strengthens immune system, prevents cancer, reduces radiation damage, forcing spleen, dissolves stagnation. Relieves constipation, strengthens mother milk
Cooking time approx. 1 1/2 hours
Calories p. portion: 138
8 portions
Allergens: AGL

Quantity of ingredients
Basil (fresh) 1 Bunch / 125g. (yes)
Salt 1 pinch / 2g. (little)
Pepper (ground) 1 pinch / 1g. (yes)
Basic recipe for a vegetable soup (nutritious) 3 lbs / 1250g. (yes)
Celery root 1/4 lbs - 4oz / 100g. (yes)
Parmesan 1 oz / 30g. (yes)

Potato 1/4 lbs - 4oz / 100g. (yes)
Broccoli 5/8 oz / 200g. (yes)
Fennel 1 piece / 250g. (yes)
Thyme dried 1/2 teaspoon / 2g. (yes)
Toast bread (whole grain) 1 slice / 5g. (yes)
Olive oil 2 table spoons / 30g. (yes)
Carrot 3/8 lbs - 6oz / 150g. (yes)
Tomato 5/8 oz / 200g. (yes)
Garlic 1 clove / 5g. (yes)
Oregano dried 1 teaspoon / 3g. (yes)
Onion (spring onion) 4 pieces / 80g. (yes)
Peas, green 1/8 lbs - 2oz / 50g. (yes)
Bay leaf 1 piece / 0,5g. (yes)
Oregano dried 1/2 teaspoon / 2g. (yes)

Cooking instructions:
Sauce:
Tear off tomatoes and cut into small pieces. Reduce in a pot with a little olive oil, finely chopped garlic. Add 1 slice of dry toasted bread (crumbed), fresh finely grated Parmesan, finely chopped basil, oregano, salt and pepper.

Soup:
Boil the vegetable broth according to the basic recipe, add coarsely sliced carrots, diced celery, diced potatoes, small florets, broccoli, finely chopped fennel tuber, peas, thyme, oregano and the bay leaf. let cook 10 minutes.

Cut 4 scallions into thin rings, add them and cook another 2 min.

Pour sauce into a soup bowl. First only a few tablespoons. Stir boiling broth with it, then stir in the soup little by little.

9.111   Vegetable juice

Promotes digestion, helps to digest fat, supports urination, reduces blood pressure, strengthens immune system, prevents cancer, reduces radiation damage, forcing spleen, is stimulating.
Cooking time approx. 15 min
Calories p. portion: 64
1 portions
Allergens: L

Quantity of ingredients
Celery root 1/2 oz / 20g. (yes)
Carrot 1/4 lbs - 4oz / 100g. (yes)
Salt 1 teaspoon / 2g. (little)
Acerola fruit nectar or powder 1/2 teaspoon / 1g. (little)
Garlic 1 piece / 2g. (yes)
Tomato 1/4 lbs - 4oz / 100g. (yes)

Cooking instructions:
Peel all ingredients and use the juicer to make a drink. Stir in the acerola.

9.112 Vegetable semolina soup

Diuretic, harmonizes the stomach and intestines, conducts bowel winds, reduces blood pressure, lowers cholesterol, detoxifying, good to fight loss of appetite, flatulence, inflammatory bowel disease, heartburn, twelffinger intestinal ulcers. Stimulates digestion, reduces pain.
Cooking time approx. 20 min
Calories p. portion: 199
3 portions
Allergens: AEGL

Quantity of ingredients
Basic recipe for a vegetable soup (nutritious) 2 cup / 500g. (yes)
Potato 1 piece / 80g. (yes)
Kohlrabi 1/2 piece / 200g. (yes)
Butter Bio 1 table spoon / 20g. (little)
Celery root 3/8 lbs - 6oz / 150g. (yes)
Lovage 1/2 teaspoon / 2g. (yes)
Carrot 1 piece / 120g. (yes)
Soy sauce 1 teaspoon / 3g. (yes)
Beans (green, fresh) 1/4 lbs / 100g. (yes)
Wheat semolina 2 table spoons / 24g. (yes)
Parsnip 1 piece / 180g. (yes)

Cooking instructions:
Worm the prepared vegetable soup; cook the vegetables in the soup softly. Spread some wheatgrass and let it swell. At the end, add lovage-green and a little butter and taste with soy sauce.

9.113   Warming carrot soup

Strengthens and warms, reduces blood pressure, strengthens immune system, prevents cancer, reduces radiation damage, strengthens gastrointestinal function.
Cooking time approx. 30 min
Calories p. portion: 133
3 portions
Allergens: HL

Quantity of ingredients
Basic recipe for a vegetable soup (nutritious) 2 cup / 500g. (yes)
Carrot 4 pieces / 250g. (yes)
Walnut oil 2 table spoons / 20g. (yes)
Onion (shallot) 2 pieces / 40g. (yes)
Anise (Common Fennel) 1/2 teaspoon / 1g. (yes)
Nutmeg 1 pinch / 1g. (yes)
Ginger fresh 1/2 teaspoon / 1g. (yes)
Parsley 1 table spoon / 10g. (yes)
Salt 1 pinch / 1g. (little)

Cooking instructions:
Heat walnut oil in a hot pot and fry onions; steam the carrots in it; add anise, nutmeg, a little ginger, salt and sauté everything; add water or vegetable- or meat stock; cook everything soft and then puree; fold in parsley at the end.

Recommendation: Suitable for the cold season, especially if you use meat broth as a liquid for infusion.

9.114   Wheat semolina with olives-herb-sauce and salad

Protects the digestive system. Detoxifying, affects anorexia, good to fight flatulence, inflammatory bowel disease, obesity, gout, stomach ulcers, stomach cramps, rheumatism, heartburn. Dissolves stagnation, relieves
Cooking time approx. 15 min
Calories p. portion: 245
3 portions
Allergens: ACGL

Quantity of ingredients
Lettuce 2 handful / 30g. (yes)
Oregano fresh 1 teaspoon / 2g. (yes)
Lemon juice 1 teaspoon / 3g. (yes)
Olive oil 1 teaspoon / 3g. (yes)
Water 1/3 cup / 65g. (yes)
Chives 1 table spoon / 7g. (yes)
Olive oil 1 teaspoon / 2g. (yes)
Onion white 1 piece / 60g. (yes)
Lemon peel 1 pinch / 1g. (yes)
Pepper (ground) 1 pinch / 0,5g. (yes)
Wheat semolina 1/4 lbs - 4oz / 100g. (yes)
Cream, sweet 30% 1/8 lbs - 2oz / 40g. (little)
Basic recipe for a vegetable soup (nutritious) 2 cups / 500g. (yes)
Chicken egg 1 piece / 60g. (little)

Cooking instructions:
Mix cream and water and heat till it boils. Stir in the wheat semolina and cook to a thick porridge and remove from heat. Whisk the egg and stir in, season with pepper and grated lemon zest. Form with 2 coffee spoons, dumplings and leave to stir in the slightly boiling vegetable stock until the dumplings float up.
Chop the onion and roast it in olive oil in a pan. Pour the semolina dumplings into the pan and sprinkle with finely chopped chives.
Wash salad and cut into thin strips. Season with olive oil, lemon juice and oregano.

9.115   Wild garlic cream soup

Reduces blood pressure, strengthens immune system, good to fight acute or chronic constipation. Improves the flow characteristics of the blood.
Cooking time approx. 15 min
Calories p. portion: 232
4 portions
Allergens: GL

Quantity of ingredients
Salt 1 pinch / 1g. (little)
Wild garlic (garlic spinach) 5/8 lbs - 8oz / 250g. (yes)
Onion (spring onion) 2 pieces / 40g. (yes)
Cream (30% fat) 5/8 lbs - 8oz / 250g. (little)
Basic recipe for a vegetable soup (nutritious) 3 cups / 750g. (yes)

Cooking instructions:
Wash the wild garlic leaves and dry them carefully. Cut the wild garlic leaves into fine strips. (Dried wild garlic: Leave approx. 80g in 40g of water for 10 minutes.)
Shortly fry the wild garlic with the finely diced onion in hot butter, deglaze with the vegetable stock and simmer over medium heat for 10 minutes. Then puree the soup, refine with whipped cream and season with salt.

9.116   Wild garlic dumplings

Improves the flow characteristics of the blood, reduces blood pressure, lowers cholesterol.
Cooking time approx. 30 min
Calories p. portion: 906
4 portions
Allergens: ACG

Quantity of ingredients
Nutmeg 1 pinch / 0,5g. (yes)
Pepper (ground) 1 pinch / 0,5g. (yes)
Salt 1 pinch / 1g. (little)
Tomato 5/8 oz / 200g. (yes)
Parmesan 1/8 lbs - 2oz / 50g. (yes)
Sugar white 1 pinch / 1g. (little)
Butter (half fat) 1/2 oz / 10g. (little)
Onion white 1 piece / 50g. (yes)
Chicken yolk 2 pieces / 20g. (little)
Potato (mealy) 1,1 lbs / 500g. (yes)
Wild garlic (garlic spinach) 5/8 oz / 200g. (yes)
Olive oil 1 table spoon / 10g. (yes)
Butter (half fat) 1/8 lbs - 2oz / 40g. (little)
Turkey ham 5/8 lbs - 8oz / 250g. (little)
Wheat semolina 1/8 lbs - 2oz / 50g. (yes)
Wheat flour 3/8 lbs - 6oz / 150g. (yes)

Cooking instructions:
Boil potatoes in salted water, peel and squeeze through the press while still hot.
Fresh wild garlic: wash, clean and briefly dive into sparkling boiling salt water (blanch). Quench cold and express.
Coarsely chop the wild garlic.
Dried wild garlic: Leave approx. 100g wild garlic in 100g of water for 10

minutes and use with the water.

Melt 50g of the butter. Mix flour, semolina, egg yolks and liquid butter with the potato mixture, knead in wild garlic. Season with salt and pepper and grated nutmeg and let rest for about 15 minutes.

Peel onion, finely chop and fry in the remaining butter. Add chopped tomatoes, simmer for a few minutes, season with salt and pepper and sugar.

Make 3 dumplings per person from the potato mixture. Soak in salted water for about 15 minutes.

In the meantime, lightly fry the ham in oil. Rub the cheese. Drain the dumplings, serve with the ham, the tomato sauce and grated cheese.

9.117   Wild garlic-scrambled eggs-breads

Calms nerves and stomach, improves the flow characteristics of the blood, good to fight constipation.
Cooking time approx. 10 min
Calories p. portion: 360
2 portions
Allergens: AC

Quantity of ingredients
Salt 1 pinch / 1g. (little)
Pepper (ground) 1 pinch / 0,5g. (yes)
Chicken egg 4 pieces / 240g. (little)
Wild garlic (garlic spinach) 1/4 lbs - 4oz / 120g. (yes)
Whole grain bread 6 pieces / 150g. (recommended)

Cooking instructions:
Fresh wild garlic: Wash the wild garlic leaves and dry them carefully. Cut the wild garlic leaves into fine strips.
Dried wild garlic: Leave approx. 80g in 40g of water for 10 minutes.
Heat the oil in a frying pan, froth the eggs and stir in the wild garlic, salt and pepper. Pour into the pan and stir until the egg has dissolved from the pan and forms fine lumps. Arrange on wholemeal bread slices.

10 Effects of food

10.1 Use ingredients: recommendable

Acai powder
Aloe juice
Amaranth
Apricot
Apricots
Bamboo shoots
Bitter Herb liqueur
Black beans
Black-eyed peas
Boletus mushroom
Boxhorn clover seeds
Broad beans (thick beans)
Buckwheat
Buckwheat whole grain
Buttermilk
Cauliflower
Channa-Dal
Chard
Chickpeas
Cream 10% coffee cream
Fig
Fig dried
Fox nut, gorgon nut, makhana
French beans
Green spelt
Hibiscus
Juniper berry
Kefir
Kidney beans (red)
Kudzu
Lentils
Lentils black
Lentils red
Lentils yellow
Lily bulbs
Lima beans
Linseed
Linseed (crushed)
Manioc flour
Mascarpone cheese
Millet
Millet flakes

Muesli
Multi-grain bread (gray bread)
Mung bean
Mung bean sprouting
Noodles (whole grain) with egg
Oat
Oat flakes (whole grain)
Oat flakes roasted
Oat meal
Papaya
Pinto beans speckled
Plum
Plum dried
Plums
Pomegranate
Psyllium seed
Red cabbage
Rice (whole grain)
Rye wholemeal bread
Sauerkraut (cutted cabbage fermented)
Savoy cabbage / kale
Sesame, black
Sesame, white
Sorrel
Sour milk
Soya Cuisine (soy cream)
Soybeans
Soybeans, black
Soybeans, blacks, fermented
Soybeans, yellow
Spelled (Dark) bread
Spelled wholemeal flour
Sunflower seeds
Wax gourd
Wheat bran
Wheat flour whole grain
Wheat/Rye/Gray-black bread with yeast
White beans
White cabbage
Whole grain bread
Wholemeal flour
Zucchini

10.2 Use ingredients: yes

Adzuki beans
Agar agar (kelp)
Agrimony
Almond

Amaranth Pops
Anchovy / Sardine
Angelica root
Anise (Common Fennel)

Apricot dried
Arrowroot
Artichoke
Asparagus (green or white)
Aubergine
Avocado
Baking powder
Balm
Banchatee (green tea)
barberry
Barley
Barley flour
Barley grass powder
Barley grouts
Barley malt
Barley not peeled
Basic recipe for a beef soup
Basic recipe for a beef soup (warming)
Basic recipe for a chicken soup (warming)
Basic recipe for a duck soup
Basic recipe for a fish soup
Basic recipe for a vegetable soup (nutritious)
Basil
Basil (fresh)
Batavia
Bay leaf
Beans (green, fresh)
Bearberry leaf
Berries of the season
Berry juice
Bitter Lemon
Bitter orange peel
Black caraway
Black fungus mushroom
Blackberry leaves
Blackberry´s
Blackthorn (Sloe)
Blue mallow tee
Blueberry
Bocksdorn fruits (Fructus Lycii, Goji, goji berry dried
Borage
Brazil nuts
Bread with carob kernel flour
Broccoli
Brussels sprouts
Buckbean
Buckwheat (roasted) Kasha
Bulgur (cereals)
Burdock root tea
Bush beans
Butter beans white

Calamari
Cantaloupe
Capers in olive oil
Carambola (Star fruit)
Cardamom
Carob flour, St. john's bread
Carrot
Carrot (Early Carrot)
Carrot juice without sugar
Cashews
Caviar
Celery root
Celery sticks
Cereal coffee
Chamomile
Chamomile tea
Champignon
Chanterelle
Chenpi (chinese tangerine bowl)
Cherry
Cherry (sour)
Cherry compote
Cherry juice
Chervil
Chervil dried
Chestnut puree
Chestnuts
Chicory
Chili (pod or ground)
Chinese cabbage
Chinese pearl barley
Chives
Chlorella (fresh water)
Chrysanthemum blossom tea
Cinnamon ground
Cinnamon sticks
Clementine
Clementines
Clove
Cocoa
Coconut milk
Cod
Codfish
Coffee
Coix (seeds) YiYi Ren
Compote (fruits of the season)
Coriander
Coriander (fresh)
Corn
Corn (fast polenta)
Corn (roasted)
Corn Grease (Polenta)
Corn silk tea
Cottage cheese

Couscous
Cow's milk (1.5% fat)
Cow's milk (whole milk 3.5% fat)
Crab
Cranberries
Cranberry
Cranberry
Cranberry jam
Cranberry juice
Cream sour 10%
Cream sour 20%
Creamer
Cress
Crispbread
Crucian
Cucumber
Cucumber (bitter)
Cucumber (spicy cucumber)
Cumin (Caraway seed)
Curcuma
Curd cheese 20%
Currant (black)
Currant (red)
Currant (white)
Currant jam (black)
Currant jam (red)
Currant juice (black)
Curry
Curry paste red
Daisy
Dandelion (young plants)
Dandelion juice
Dandelionroots tea
Dashi
Dates dried
Dates red
Dill
Dulse (seaweed)
Dyer's broom herb
Edam cheese
Eel
Eel smoked
Elderberries
Elderberry blossom tee
Endive salad
Fennel
Fennel seeds ground
Fennel tea
Fenugreek (Trigonella foenum-graecum)
Feta cheese
Feta cheese
Fish pieces mixed (fresh water)
Fish remains

Fish sauce
Flounder
Flower pollen
Fresh cheese
Fresh cheese from soya
Fresh cheese with herbs
Freshwater crab
Freshwater fish
Fruit mix juice
Fruit tea
Gail plum
Galangal
Garam Masala powder
Garlic
Gelatin white
Gelee Royal
Gentian root
Gentian root tea
Ginger fresh
Ginger powder
Ginkgo fruit
Ginseng
Ginseng root
Goat
Goat and sheep's milk
Goat cheese
Gooseberry
Gouda cheese
Gourd
Grape juice red
Grape juice white
Grapefruit (Pomelo)
Grapefruit dried peel
Grapefruit juice
Grapes red
Grapes white
Green tea
Greengage
Ground
Ground caraway
Guava
Halibut (Flatfish)
Hawthorn
Hazelnuts
Herbal tea mix
Herbs bitter
Herbs of Provence
Herbs various
Herbs wild
Herring
Hibiscus tea
Hijiki
Hokkaido pumpkin
Hop

93

Horehound leaves
Hyssop
Iceberg lettuce
Jasmine blossoms tee
Jellyfish
Kaki plum
Kalmus
King Solomon's-seal
Kiwi
Kohlrabi
Kombu seaweed (Saccharina japonica)
Kukicha tea
Kumquats
Lamb's lettuce
Lamb's lettuce
Lavender blossoms
Leaf salads (bitter)
Leek
Lemon
Lemon Balm (dried)
Lemon Balm (fresh)
Lemon juice
Lemon peel
Lemongrass
Lettuce
Licorice root tea
Lime
Lime blossom tea
Linseed oil
Liver smoothing tea
Lobster
Longane
Loquate / Japanese medlar
Lotus roots
Lotus seeds
Lovage
Lovage seeds
Luo Han Guo fruit
Lychee
Lychee in Preserved
Lye roll
Mackerel
Mallow (Malva sylvestris) blossom tea
Malt
Mango
Mare's milk
Marjoram
Mediterranean fish (cod, plaice, haddock, sea eel, mackerel)
Medlar

Mirabelle plum
Miso
Miso black (fermented)

Miso paste (soy bean paste)
Mixed Pickles
Mold cheese
Morel (black, dried)
Morel, dried
Mozzarella
Mu Erh Mushroom
Mulberry fruit
Mulled Wine Spice
Mullet
Mussels
Mustard
Mustard Dijon
Mustard medium hot
Mustard seeds
Mustard sweet
Nasturtium (nose-twister or nose-tweaker)
Nectarine
Nettles
Nori, purple seaweed, red algae
Nutmeg
Oat flour
Oat fusion (baby food)
Oat milk
Octopus
Octopus
Okra
Olive oil
Olives
Olives green
Onion (shallot)
Onion (spring onion)
Onion read
Onion white
Orange
Orange blossom
Orange dried peel
Orange grated peel
Orange peel
Oregano dried
Oregano fresh
Oyster mushroom
Oyster shell powder
Parmesan
Parsley
Parsley root
Parsnip
Passion blossoms tea
Passion fruit
Peaches
Peaches (canned)
Peanuts
Pear

Pear juice
Pearl barley
Pearl barley
Peas
Peas, green
Pepper (ground)
Pepper Cayenne
Pepper powder (hot)
Pepper white (ground)
Peppercorns
Peppermint
Peppermint tea
Pepperoni
Pepperoni, red, pitted, halved
Pepperoni, yellow, pitted, halved
Peppers
Peppers (rose peppers)
Peppers (sweet)
Peppers powder
Perch
Pickle
Pimento
Pine nuts
Pineapple
Pineapple (from a can)
Pineapple juice without sugar
Pistachios
Plaice
Poppy
Potato
Potato (mealy)
Potato flour
Prickly pear
Processed cheese 12%
processed cheese 30%
Pudding powder vanilla
Pumpernickel (dark bread)
Pumpkin
Pumpkin seeds
Quail
Quince
Quinoa
Radicchio
Radish
Radish (white, green, purple-red)
Radish black
Radish horseradish
Radish leaves
Rapeseed oil
Raspberry
Raspberry dried (immature)
Raspberry leaf tea
Red beet
Red berry (without sugar)

Reishi mushroom
Rhubarb
Ribworttea
Rice mash
Rice wild (nature rice)
Romaine lettuce / lettuce salad
Rose blossom tea
Rose hip
Rose hip tea
Rose leaf tea
Rosefish
Rosemary
Rucola
Rye
Rye flour
Safflower (Dyer's thistle / Hong Hua)
Saffron
Sage
Sago (cereals)
Sake
Salmon
Salsify
Savory
Sea buckthorn
Sea cucumber
Seacrab
Sesame paste (Tahini)
Shark
Sheep's milk
Sheep's milk yoghurt
Shiitake, dried
Shrimp
Shrimps
Skim milk powder
Slug
Sour cherries
Sour cream 15% fat
Sour milk cheese 20%
Sourdough
Soy flour
Soy noodles
Soy sauce
Soy Tofu
Soy Tofu smoked
Soybean milk
Spelled flakes
Spelled grain
Spelled semolina
Spinach
Spiny lobsters
Spurdog (spiny dogfish, Schillerlocken)
St. Benedict's thistle, blessed thistle, holy thistle, spotted thistle
Star anise

Stevia (candyleaf, sweetleaf)
Strawberries
Strawberry Juice
Sugar substitute (sweetener)
Sweet potato
Tabasco
Tangerine
Tarragon (Estragon)
Tea mixture uric acid lowering
Thyme
Thyme dried
Toast bread (whole grain)
Tomato
Tomato dried
Tomato juice
Tomato paste
Tomato puree
Tonic Water
Topinambur
Trout
Trout (smoked)
Truffle
Tsampa (roasted barley flour)
Tuna
Turmeric (yellow root)
Turnip
Turnips
Umeboshi paste
Umeboshi plums (Japanese apricots)
Valerian
Vanilla
Vanilla pod
Vanilla powder
Vegetable juice
Vinegar (Apple vinegar)
Vinegar (Red wine vinegar)
Vinegar Aceto Balsamico
Vinegar Aceto Balsamico white
Wakame
Walnut oil
Walnuts
Walnuts roasted
Water
Water hot
Watermelon
Wheat
Wheat bulgur
Wheat flakes
Wheat flour
Wheat semolina
Wheat semolina for children
Wheatgrass juice
Wheatgrass powder
Whey
Whitefish
Wild boar meat
Wild garlic (garlic spinach)
Wild herbs
Wild strawberries
Wormwood
Wormwood herb
Yam root, yam root tuber
Yarrow
Yarrow tea
Yew nut
Yoghurt vanilla
Yogi tea
Yogurt (natural, 1.5% fat)
Yogurt (natural, 3.5% fat)

10.3 Use ingredients: little

Acerola fruit nectar or powder
Agave nectar
Almond marzipan
Almond milk
Almond puree
Apple (sour)
Apple (sweet)
Apple juice (natural cloudy)
Apple puree
Apricot jam
Apricot nectar
Apricots juice
Bean oil
Beef bone marrow
Beef fillet
Beef heart
Beef heart (calf)
Beef kidney
Beef liver
Beef lungs (calf)
Beef meat
Beef meat (calf)
Beef meatbones
Beef Oxtail pieces
Beef soup meat
Beef stomach
Beer (alcohol-free)
Beer (alcohol-reduced)
Beer (Pils)
Beer (Top-fermented German dark

beer)
Bitter liqueur
Blackberry dried (unripe fruit)
Blackberry jam
Blueberry jam
Blueberry juice
Borage oil
Bread roll
Brie cheese
Brown ale
Butter (half fat)
Butter Bio
Camembert
Campari
Carp
Chicken Blood
Chicken egg
Chicken egg white
Chicken heart
Chicken liver
Chicken meat
Chicken stomach
Chicken yolk
Chickweed
Clarified butter
Coconut fat
Coconut flakes
Coconut grated
Coconut meat
Cola drink
Cola drink (low calorie)
Cooking oil
Corn flour
Corn germ oil
Corn starch
Cream (30% fat)
Cream sour 30%
Cream, sweet 30%
Creme fraiche cheese
Curd cheese 40%
Currants (black)
Currants (red)
Deer meat
Deer meat
Deer's Bones
Deer's kidneys
Duck (heart)
Duck (slaughtered)
Ducks egg
Emmental cheese
Evening primrose oil
Fernet Branca (herbal bitter liqueur)
Fish innards
Fructose (glucose)

Ginger oil
Ginseng liqueur
Goat and sheep's blood
Goat and sheep's brain
Goat and sheep's liver
Goat and sheep's stomach
Goose
Goose blood
Goose egg
Goose fat
Goose parts
Gorgonzola
Grapeseed oil
Grass carp
Honey
Honey wine (Met)
Horse meat
Ladyfingers
Lamb bones
Lamb kidneys
Lamb liver
Lamb meat
Lamb shoulder
Lychee liqueur
Mango juice
Maple syrup
Margarine
Margarine (diet)
Martini
Mayonnaise 50%
Mayonnaise 80%
Mineral water
Mutton
Mutton
Noodles (wheat) with egg
Noodles (wheat, lasagne) with egg
Noodles (wheat, ribbon noodles) with egg
Noodles (wheat, spaghetti) with egg
Orange jam
Orange juice
Oysters
Palm oil
Peanut (roasted)
Peanut butter
Peanut oil
Pheasant
Pig blood
Pigeon
Pigeon egg
Pork Bacon
Pork brain
Pork ham
Pork ham cooked

Pork ham smoked
Pork heart
Pork kidneys
Pork knuckle
Pork Lard
Pork liver
Pork lung
Pork marrow bones
Pork meat
Pork sausage (Bratwurst)
Pork skin
Pork stomach
Pork/beef sausage (smoked)
Pork's intestine
Prosecco
Pumpkin seed oil
Quail egg
Rabbit
Rabbit (wild)
Rabbit liver
Rabbit meat
Raisins
Raspberry jam
Red wine
Rice (fragrance)
Rice (Gaoliang / Sorghum)
Rice Basmati
Rice black
Rice flour
Rice long grain rice
Rice malt
Rice noodles
Rice red

Rice sticky
Rice variety any
Rum
Rusk
Salt
Salt (herbal)
Sesame oil
Sesame oil roasted
Sherry (whine)
Soybean oil
Spirit
Strawberry jam
Sugar - icing sugar
Sugar brown
Sugar candy white
Sugar cane sugar
Sugar fructose - fruit sugar
Sugar glucose - grapes sugar
Sugar Milk Sugar
Sugar molasses
Sugar palm sugar
Sugar white
Sunflower oil
Thistle oil
Turkey breast meat
Turkey ham
Vanilla sugar natural
Wheat beer
Wheat flatbread/pita bread
Wheat germ oil
White wine
Yeast

10.4 Do not use contra-acting foods

Banana
Banana (cooking banana)
Basic recipe for a rice soup (Congee)
Black tea
Blueberry dried
Breadcrumbs (wheat bread, bread roll)
Chocolate
Chocolate (Diabetic)
Pork fat (lard)
Puff pastry

Rice round grain
Rice starch
Rice sweet
Supplementary nutrition
White bread (baguette)
White bread (pretzel sticks)
White bread (roll)
White bread (wheat bread)
White breadcrumbs
White dumpling bread (wheat bread)

11 Herbs and their effects

11.1 Basil (fresh)

It has a beneficial effect on flatulence and nausea, relaxing and soothing. Good to fight amphysema, bronchitis, whooping cough, high blood pressure, headache, mouth odor, warts, hiccup, gout, migraine.

11.2 Savory

Stomach-strengthening, soothing and appetizing. Ideal for prevent colds, strengthens the immune system. In case of incontinence or nocturnal wetting (not for children), put the beans in liquor for libido.

11.3 Nettles

Promotes urination. Tea or juice, cleanses the blood and the kidneys, supports prostate problems, inhibit the formation of inflammation, pain-relieving.

11.4 Dill

The medicinal and spice herb has an antispasmodic effect and stimulates gastric juice production. Good to fight flatulence. Antispasmodic for gastrointestinal discomfort.

11.5 Chervil dried

Forces urination, detoxifying, blood-purifying and blood-pressure-reducing effects.

11.6 Coriander

The essential oils are appetizing, digestive, cramping and soothing in stomach and intestinal disorders.

11.7 Herbs various

Appetizing, lots of trace elements and vitamins

11.8 Cress

Diuretic, supports urination. Good to fight dry mouth, inner agitation, sore throat, diabetes, kidney stones, gastrointestinal complaints, lung problems, menstrual cramps or cancer.

11.9 Chives

Bactericide, prevents cancer, strengthens gastric juice production, promotes digestion and blood circulation, promotes growth, triggers stagnation.

11.10 Lovage

Stimulates digestion, reduces pain. Extracts of the root are used to flush out urinary tract infections and prevent kidney gravel.

11.11 Dandelion (young plants)

Detoxifies, relieves inflammation. Regulates digestion, helps with rheumatism, releases kidney stones, leaves pimples and chronic skin disorders disappear.

11.12 Marjoram

Helps to digest fat foods, strengthens digestive organs, helps to fight colds, strengthens menstruation, promotes skin healing.

11.13 Oregano fresh

It has an anti-digestive, calming and nerve-strengthening effect, helps to fight cramping stomach and intestinal disorders. The ingredient Carvacrol has an anti-inflammatory effect.

11.14 Parsley

Stimulates liver function, detoxifies. Forces urinating. Relieves flatulence. Digestive and menstrual stimulating, birth-accelerating, memory-enhancing, blood-purifying, skin-smoothing.

11.15 Peppermint

Relaxes, frees the lungs and the nose (inhale), regulates the cycle. Stimulates bile flow and bile production, antispasmodic in gastrointestinal disorders, antimicrobial and antiviral.

11.16 Rosemary

Promotes digestion, relieves bloating, strengthens lung, spleen and kidney. Affects the circulation and nerves. Appetizing. Baths help to fight circulatory disorders as well as with gout and rheumatism.

11.17 Sage

Good to fight yeast infections. The leaves have a digestive effect and are used in greasy foods. Antiperspirant effect. Helps to relieve coughing attacks. Dries out (TCM).

11.18 Sorrel

Astringent, hematopoietic, purifies the blood, diuretic. Good to fight liver weakness, upset stomach, indigestion, constipation, diarrhea, worms, scurvy, anemia, women's complaints, wounds, skin rashes, boils, ulcers, swelling.

11.19 Blackthorn (Sloe)

The blossoms, bark and fruits are astringent, diuretic, weakly laxative, fever-shedding, stomach-enhancing and anti-inflammatory.

11.20 Black caraway

Detoxifying, immunoregulatory. In addition, the oil should stimulate the formation of bone marrow cells and generally protect body cells from viruses.

11.21 Thyme dried

Disinfecting. It stimulates the blood circulation, increases the appetite and helps to digest fat meat better. Strengthens lungs and spleen (TCM).

11.22 Lemongrass

Reduction of flatulence, antimicrobial, appetizing. Prevention of influenza. Good to fight infections in the mouth and throat.

11.23 Lemon Balm (fresh)

Stimulating, antibacterial, encouraging, relaxing, antispasmodic, cooling, antipyretic, analgesic, sweat-inducing, virus-inhibiting. Good for colds, fever, flu, cough, bronchitis, asthma, loss of appetite, bloating, heartburn.

12 Basics of Nutrition

The basic principles of nutrition described herein are general recommendations. They are not aimed at a specific form of therapy. Recommendations concerning a therapy have priority.

12.1 Nutrition

Regular meals in a relaxed atmosphere. A warm breakfast is considered a good start into the day.
The main meals ought to be taken for lunch – supper in the early evening. Pay attention to feeling hungry or sated: don't eat too much nor remain hungry is the rule
Prepare the meals freshly from natural, regional products. Frozen, heat-conserved, industrially prepared or foodstuffs cooked in the microwave oven are rejected.
Choice of foodstuffs according to the season: more cooling food in summer, more warming food in winter.
Eat cooked food at least twice a day. Food and drinks ought to be lukewarm, never ice-cold or hot.
Raw vegetables, briefly cooked vegetables, freshly squeezed juices and mineral water are not recommended. Milk and dairy products are only included in the diet if they don't cause problems.
Don't use therapeutic recipes over a longer period without consulting your doctor or therapist.

Varied food
Enjoy the diversity of foodstuffs. Characteristics of a balanced nutrition are variety, suitable combination and a balanced quantity of rich and low energy foodstuffs (on one hand avoiding undersupply with essential nutrients and on the other hand to take to many undesirable substances).

A lot of Cereal Products - and Potatoes
Bread, pasta, rice, cereal flakes (best wholemeal) as well as potatoes contain almost no fat, but many vitamins, mineral nutrients, trace elements, roughage and secondary plant substances. These foodstuffs ought to be taken with low-fat side dishes.

Vegetables and Fruit – „Take Five" every day ...
5 portions of vegetables and fruit a day, as fresh as possible, briefly cooked, or maybe one portion as a juice – ideal as a side dish to every meal as well as snack between meals: Thus a lot of vitamins, mineral nutrients as well as roughage and secondary plant substances

Daily milk and dairy products
Milk and Dairy Products every Day, once or twice per Week Fish; meat, sausages as well as eggs moderately. These foodstuffs contain valuable nutrients like calcium in the milk, iodine selenium and omega-3 fat acids in saltwater fish. Meat is favorable due to its high content of disposable iron and the vitamins B1, B6 and B12. Quantities of 300 – 600 g meat and sausage per week are sufficient. Prefer low-fat products, especially in meat- and dairy products.

Low-fat and fatty Foodstuffs
Fat supplies us with essential fat acids and fatty foodstuffs contain also fat-soluble vitamins. Fat is high in energy; therefore much fat in the food may cause overweight, possibly also cancer. Too many saturated fat acids may further a tendency for cardio-vascular diseases in the long term. Prefer vegetable oils and fats (e.g. rapeseed-, olive-, soya-oils and solid fats produced therefrom). Beware of invisible fat in meat- and dairy products, pastry and sweets as well as in fast-food and convenience foods. 70 – 90 g fat per day is sufficient.

Moderately Sugar and Salt
Take sugar and foods/drinks containing various kinds of sugar (e.g. glucose syrup) only occasionally. Use herbs and spices as well as a little salt creatively. Prefer salt containing iodine.

Plenty of Liquids
Water is absolutely essential. Drink 1-2 l liquids every day. Prefer water (with or without gas) and other low-calorie drinks. Alcoholic drinks should not be taken.

Tasty Dishes, carefully cooked
Cook the meals with as low temperatures and as short as possible, using little water and fat – this preserves the original taste, keeps the nutrients intact and prevents the production of harmful compounds.

Take time and enjoy the food
Take your Time and enjoy your Food
Eating consciously helps to eat right. The eye enjoys food, too. It's fun, invites to enjoy varied dishes and stimulates the feeling of satiety.

Watch your Weight and stay in Motion
A balanced diet and a lot of exercise and sport (30 – 60 min/day) are a healthy combination. The right weight furthers well-being and health. Thermals, directional effectiveness, digestive power

There are various criteria for judging the effectiveness of herbs and foodstuffs.

The use of certain herbs and ingredients is based on observations of the effects on the body which these foodstuffs, herbs and spices show after having eaten them. The medical science has developed following system: Every ingredient or herb has a directional effectiveness. Furthermore, there are herbs which have a special effect on certain organs.

The basic condition for a healthy metabolism is to obtain sufficient energy from food and that the digestive process doesn't use too much energy. An easily digestible meal makes content and sated, doesn't cause flatulence and fatigue after the meal. The perfect spices increase the healthiness of our meals. Very often, just small doses of herbs and spices will suffice. They are not used to make us sated, but to help our digestive organs to digest the food.

12.2 Recipes

The recipes list the ingredients to be used and the cooking instructions show how the dish is prepared. The list of ingredients shows the concerned quantities as well as the relevance for the therapy. If you find „less than mentioned", try to comply or find an alternative from the „list of recommended foodstuffs". Mostly it shall result just in a small change of taste when you simply avoid this ingredient.

Mild cooking methods: boiling, stewing, poaching, steaming
Strong cooking methods: barbecuing, roasting, frying, smoking
Balanced cooking methods: deep-frying, baking brick
Deep-freezing and warming in the microwave oven should be avoided (denaturalization).

12.3 Foodstuffs

Foodstuffs have an effect on body and soul like medicinal herbs, only a very much milder one. Dietary advice is mainly based on regional foodstuffs. The knowledge about the effects of each foodstuff and the knowledge, when which foodstuff shall be used, is based on the orthodox school of medicine. Use ecologic-organic products, if possible. As everything should be cooked for a long time due to a better digestability and very rarely eaten raw, the food agrees with everyone.

The classification of the foodstuffs according to their effect on the body is the basis in order to achieve a harmonious status of health.

Dietary advisors do not recommend certain foodstuffs for everyone. The individual diet is tailor-made for the individual constitution.

Buy only fresh and ripe fruit and vegetables. You ought to leave unripe fruit and vegetables and such with brown spots and wilted leaves behind in the market. In this case take deep-frozen goods (never ready-to-serve dishes!). Fruit and vegetables are deep-frozen immediately after harvesting and often contain more vitamins and minerals than the goods from the vegetable shelf. Whereas conserved or tinned goods contain very much less biological substances. Also, salt, sugar and others are mostly added to the latter. Never leave the foodstuffs in the water after washing them to avoid that many vital substances get drowned. Clean salads, fruit and vegetables immediately before serving.

Please make sure of the hygienic processing of foodstuffs. Clean your salads, fruit and vegetables carefully. When cooking with meat, prepare all ingredients first and then process the meat products. Clean the worktop and tools very carefully. Wooden surfaces ought to be treated with a mild disinfectant regularly in order to reduce germination.

Store fruit and vegetables separately, if possible. Harvested fruit and vegetables are still alive and emit e.g. ethylene gas, which makes other products ripen and age faster. Keep meat and fish in the closed packaging or store them in the fridge in closed containers.

12.4 Herbs

There are some basic rules for storing medicinal herbs. On principle, herbs must be protected from direct sunlight, humidity and heat.

Containers for the storage of herbs may be glasses, ceramic jars and even plastic containers. However, plastic is a rather unsuitable material and should only be a short-term solution. In case of glass containers, use a dark material.

Medicinal herbs cannot be kept for any long period. The shelf life of herbs is limited. However, it can be prolonged with suitable storage. The place should be dark, rather cool and absolutely dry. A wooden medicine cabinet, placed not directly next to a source of heat, would be ideal. Never buy large quantities of herbs so as not to have to throw them away. Label the container with the name of the herb and the date of harvesting or processing.

13 Other dietic-books

The following syndromes of dietetics, TCM or for a therapy supplement for cancer are available.

Dietetics

E001. Nutrition of the infant - baby food
E002. Nutrition during lactation
E003. Nutrition in old age
E004. Nutrition of children and adolescents
E005. Nutrition of athletes
E006. Light weight
E007. Pregnancy
E008. Full food

Protein and electrolyte - kidneys
E009. (hemodialysis) dialysis treatment
E010. Acute renal failure
E011. Chronic renal insufficiency
E012. Nephrotic syndrome
E013. Kidney stones (nephrolithiasis)

Gastrointestinal tract - pancreas
E014. Acute pancreatitis (inflammation of the pancreas)
E015. Chronic pancreatitis (inflammation of the pancreas)

Gastrointestinal tract - small intestine and large intestine
E016. Acute obstipation (constipation)
E017. Chronic obstipation (constipation)
E018. Colon irritabile
E019. Diverticulitis
E020. Acquired lactose intolerance (lactose malabsorption)
E021. Fructose malabsorption
E022. Glutensensitive enteropathy (celiac disease)
E023. Colectomy
E024. Short Bowel Syndrome

Gastrointestinal tract - liver, gallbladder, bile ducts
E025. Acute and chronic hepatitis (inflammation of the liver)
E026. Cholelithiasis (bile stones)
E027. fatty liver
E028. cirrhosis

Gastrointestinal tract - Stomach and duodenal intestine
E029. Acute gastritis
E030. Chronic gastritis
E031. Stomach bleeding
E032. Ulcus ventriculi and duodenal ulcer
E033. Condition after gastric surgery

Gastrointestinal tract - oral cavity and esophagus
E034. Stomatitis
E035. Esophageal carcinoma (esophageal cancer)
E036. Refluosophagitis (heartburn)

Special diseases
E037. Phenylketonuria (PKU)
E038. Rheumatic joint diseases

Metabolism
E039. Obesity (overweight)
E040. Diabetes mellitus
E041. Eating disorders (underweight)

Fat metabolism
E042. Hypercholesterolaemia (increased cholesterol level)
E043. Hepatic Encephalopathy

Heart and circulation
E044. Arteriosclerosis (arterial calcification)
E045. Heart insufficiency
E046. Hypertension
E047. Hyperuricaemia and gout

Changed nutrient requirements
E048. In case of fever
E049. For malignant diseases
E050. After burns
E051. Radiation and chemotherapy

CANCER
E100. Pancreatic cancer
E101. Bladder cancer
E102. Blood cancer (leukemia)
E103. Breast cancer
E104. Colorectal cancer
E105. Gastric cancer
E106. Kidney cancer
E107. Esophageal cancer

TCM
E200. Bladder - moisture heat in the bladder
E201. Bladder - moisture and cold in the bladder
E202. Bladder - emptiness and cold in the bladder
E203. Large intestine - external cold affects the large intestine
E204. Large intestine - moisture heat in the large intestine
E205. Large intestine - heat blocks the intestine II acute
E206. Large intestine - dryness of the colon
E207. Large intestine - Yang deficiency (cold)
E208. Heart - Blood insufficiency
E209. Heart - Blood stagnation
E210. Heart - Fire
E211. Heart - Hot mucus clogs the heart pores

E212. Heart - Cold mucus clogs the heart pores
E213. Heart - Qi deficiency
E214. Heart - Yang deficiency
E215. Heart - Yin deficiency
E216. Liver - Ascending Liver Yang
E217. Liver - Blood deficiency
E218. Liver - Blood stagnation
E219. Liver - Moisture heat in liver and gall bladder
E220. Liver - Fire
E221. Liver - Gall bladder Qi-Empty
E222. Liver - Cold in the liver meridian
E223. Liver - Qi stagnation
E224. Liver - Wind
E225. Liver - Wind with ascending liver Yang
E226. Liver - Wind with blood anemic
E227. Liver - Wind with extreme heat
E228. Lung - Qi deficiency
E229. Lung - Mucus-moisture in the lungs
E230. Lung - Mucus-heat in the lungs
E231. Lung - Mucus-cold in the lungs
E232. Lung - Dryness of the lungs
E233. Lung - Wind-heat attacks the lungs
E234. Lung - Wind-cold affects the lungs
E235. Lung - Yin deficiency
E236. Stomach - Bloodstagnation
E237. Stomach - Fire
E238. Stomach - Cold with liquid
E239. Stomach - Nutrition stagnation
E240. Stomach - Qi deficiency
E241. Stomach - Rebellious Qi
E242. Stomach - Yin Emptiness
E243. Spleen - Heat and moisture attack the spleen
E244. Spleen - Coldness and moisture affects the spleen
E245. Spleen - Qi deficiency
E246. Spleen - Qi deficiency + Declining spleen Qi
E247. Spleen - Qi deficiency + spleen does not control the blood
E248. Spleen - Yang deficiency
E249. Kidney - Heart and kidney no longer communicate
E250. Kidney - Jing deficiency
E251. Kidney - Kidneys cannot receive the Qi
E252. Kidney - Qi is not stable
E253. Kidney - Yang deficiency
E254. Kidney - Yin deficiency

For further information visit di-book.com.